S.O.S.

S.O.S.

CHILLING TALES OF ADVENTURE ON THE HIGH SEAS

EDITED BY SARA NICKLÈS

CHRONICLE BOOKS
SAN FRANCISCO

Text compilation copyright © 2001 by
Chronicle Books LLC.
All rights reserved. No part of this book
may be reproduced in any form without
written permission from the publisher.

Cover photographs copyright © Darrell
Gulin/Tony Stone; Darrell Gulin/CORBIS
Page 256 constitutes a continuation of the
copyright page.

To maintain the authentic style of each
writer included herein, quirks of spelling
and grammar remain unchanged from
their original state.

Library of Congress Cataloging-in-
Publication Data available.
ISBN 0-8118-3100-0
Printed in the United States of America

Book and Cover Design by Sara Schneider
Composition by Suzanne Scott

Distributed in Canada by
Raincoast Books
9050 Shaughnessy Street
Vancouver, British Columbia V6P 6E5

10 9 8 7 6 5 4 3 2

Chronicle Books LLC
85 Second Street
San Francisco, California 94105

www.chroniclebooks.com

FOR LOO-WEE,
THE ROGUE WAVE IN MY LIFE

CONTENTS

INTRODUCTION

Forget outer space, forget the Wild West, the ocean will always be the last frontier. It literally surrounds us, covering almost three-quarters of the earth's surface, and still it holds fast to its mysteries. The ocean has connotations of romance and adventure, but also of the unknown, the unfathomable, the mysteries of the deep. Even its maladies strike an exotic note: scurvy, mal de mer, the bends.

Most sailors will tell you that the ocean does not evoke for them these images of romance. To them, the sea is the ultimate adversary—vast, unforgiving, dangerous— the ocean that is depicted in Sebastian Junger's *The Perfect Storm*, and Joseph Conrad's *Typhoon*. But the sea inspires awe in a gentler fashion as well, as in Julia Blackburn's "The Mermaid," or Jessica Maxwell's "Rhapsody in Blue."

Along with its romantic associations for many— visions of sea spray curling over endless wave trains, or dramatic skies over infinite blue expanse—the ocean has always had a more frightening primal connection with us. Our blood shares the salt minerals and chemistry of the sea itself, and yet, in many ways, we are still profoundly ill at ease with the ocean. Perhaps innate fear of our unknowable watery origins overwhelms us, compelling us to return to the sea's terrifying and inescapable mysteries. And where there are unanswered questions, there will be tall tales to fill in the gaps.

The setting of these stories is no Gilligan's Island; this is the real ocean and its awe-inspiring vastness and all that that brings with it. Here we have the range of stories from shipwrecks, as in Stephen King's "Survivor Type," to sea monsters, like the sharks in Archibald Rutledge's "Death in the Moonlight"; stories as varied as the moods of the sea itself, including Nathaniel Philbrick's frightening account of a whale attack in *In the Heart of the Sea,* and John Biguenet's spooky story of a night in the water in "And Never Come Up."

These writers have been to sea (whether by boat, or just by pen), and have brought back these ocean tales for our vicarious thrills. For those of us who stand at the bow of the commuter ferry and imagine encounters with rogue seas, this collection provides the smell of the salt spray and the wash of the waves without getting wet.

—*Sara Nicklès*

S.O.S.°

STOR

MS

FROM **N BY E**
ROCKWELL **KENT**

In 1929 Rockwell Kent and his two companions had journeyed from Nova Scotia to Greenland on the small boat Direction *when a sudden storm descended from the ice cap beyond and heaved the* Direction *against the rocky shore.* N by E *is the story not only of the shipwreck, but also of the rebuilding of a boat and the author's wondrous discovery of Greenland.*

XLVII Lat. 63° 56' 40" N. Long. 51° 19' 00" W.

The motion woke me. Where was I? I remembered. Daylight came but faintly through the fo'castle ports, shadowed as they were by the dinghy. My clock showed ten-thirty. How I had slept!

We were rolling violently; a sudden roll, a lurch to starboard. I heard steps on deck, voices, the sound of hawser paying out. Oh, well, we're at anchor; and no one has called. I braced my knees against the side board of the bunk; I had need to.

Suddenly we were careened so far that I was almost catapulted onto the floor. I got out, dressed hastily and opened the door into the cabin. It was broad daylight there. The skipper was in bed.

"She's drifting with both anchors," called the mate from deck.

"Give 'em more rope," answered the skipper.

I reached the ladder. At that moment something rolled us over, far, far down, and held us there; and the green sea came pouring in as if to fill the ship.

"Damn it!" I cried, "and I'd made everything so neat!"

On deck a hurricane; I'd never felt such wind before. The sea was beaten flat, with every wave crest shorn and whipped to smoke; cold spray and stinging rain drove over us.

I helped the mate. "We'll need the third anchor," I said, and started aft.

The skipper appeared. "Good, get it out," he said as I passed him. I went below for the last time.

The spare anchor was knocked down and stowed under the coal sacks and provisions in the after hold; it was not easy to come at. Removing the companion ladder I set to work. Hard work it was, cramped in that narrow space on hands and knees. As I dragged the hundred pound sacks out onto the cabin floor—always, strangely, careful not to damage anything—I'd look up and see the gray sky through the opening above my head. Then one time glancing up I saw the brow of the mountain; and always after that more mountain showed and less sky. And at last the mountain side itself seemed to have moved against the ship and to be towering over it.

I had laid a lighted cigarette carefully upon the chart table; this, as I worked, was always in my mind—that it should not be left to burn the wood. And so, from time to time, I'd move it just a bit. We were so careful of our boat, to mar it in no way!

But all the while I had been shifting goods and moving sacks of coal; so that at last I came to the anchor. It was a large anchor and very heavy. I dragged it out into the cabin.

"Come," I called to the mate, "and help me get this thing on deck." And as I looked up I saw the mate in his yellow oilskins, bright against the near dark mountain side.

"Not much use now," said the mate; but he came down.

It was hard work to lift that anchor up, and we seemed not to be very strong. "I lose my strength from excitement," said the mate. I thought that I did too—but I didn't say so.

We lifted the cumbersome affair head high and tumbled it out into the cockpit. As I started to follow, a great sea lifted us and rolled us over; I hung on, half out of the cabin. And I stared straight at an oncoming wall of rock so near astern it seemed about to crush us. The sea rose high against it, and broke and became churned water that seethed around us. It cradled us and lowered us gently; and the dark land drew quietly away.

Then came another sea that hurled us and the land together. "Now for the crash!" I thought—and I gripped hard and braced myself against it, and watched the moment—thrilled by its impending horror.

There was no crash—that time. Ever so gently, just as we seemed to draw away again, our stern post touched the ledge; so lightly touched it that it made no sound, only a little tremor. And the tremor ran through the iron keel and the oak, and through the ribs and planking, and through every bolt and rail, through every fibre of the boat and us. Maybe we had not known that the end had come; now, as if God whispered it, we knew.

So for a third time we were floated back.

Then, as if the furies of the sea and wind were freed at last to end their coquetry, they lifted us—high, high above the ledge—and dropped us there. And the impact of that shock was only less than those that followed for that half an hour until *Direction* sank.

XLVIII July 15th, 10:30 to 11:00 A.M.

That half an hour! We lay, caught in the angle of a giant step of rock, keel on the tread and starboard side against the riser; held there by wind and sea; held there to lift and pound; to lift so buoyantly on every wave; to drop—crashing out thirteen iron-shod tons on granite. Lift and pound! There the perfection of our ship revealed itself; only, that having struck just once, she ever lived, a ship, to lift and strike again.

A giant sledge hammer striking a granite mountain; a hollow hammer; and within it a man. Picture yourself the man. I stayed below, and was.

See me as Adam; set full blown into that pandemonium of force, his world—of wind, storm, snow, rain, hail, lightning and thunder, earthquake and flood, hunger and cold, and the huge terrifying presence of the unknown—using his little wit toward self containedness against the too-much of immensity; and quietly—for Adam lived—doing the little first-at-hands one on another in their natural course, thinking but little and reflecting less. Adam and Man; and me in that compacted miniature of man's universe, the cabin of the yacht *Direction* on the rocks of Greenland.

We live less by imagination than despite it.

MANUSCRIPT FOUND IN A BOTTLE
EDGAR ALLAN POE

Qui n'a plus qu'un moment à vivre
N'a plus rien à dissimuler.
QUINAULT-Atys

Of my country and of my family I have little to say. Ill
usage and length of years have driven me from the one, and
estranged me from the other. Hereditary wealth afforded
me an education of no common order, and a contemplative
turn of mind enabled me to methodize the stores which
early study very diligently garnered up.—Beyond all things,
the study of the German moralists gave me great delight;
not from any ill-advised admiration of their eloquent madness, but from the ease with which my habits of rigid
thought enabled me to detect their falsities. I have often
been reproached with the aridity of my genius; a deficiency
of imagination has been imputed to me as a crime; and the
Pyrrhonism of my opinions has at all times rendered me

notorious. Indeed, a strong relish for physical philosophy has, I fear, tinctured my mind with a very common error of this age—I mean the habit of referring occurrences, even the least susceptible of such reference, to the principles of that science. Upon the whole, no person could be less liable than myself to be led away from the severe precincts of truth by the *ignes fatui* of superstition. I have thought proper to premise thus much, lest the incredible tale I have to tell should be considered rather the raving of a crude imagination, than the positive experience of a mind to which the reveries of fancy have been a dead letter and a nullity.

After many years spent in foreign travel, I sailed in the year 18—, from the port of Batavia, in the rich and populous island of Java, on a voyage to the Archipelago of the Sunda islands. I went as passenger—having no other inducement than a kind of nervous restlessness which haunted me as a fiend.

Our vessel was a beautiful ship of about four hundred tons, copper-fastened, and built at Bombay of Malabar teak. She was freighted with cotton-wool and oil, from the Lachadive islands. We had also on board coir, jaggeree, ghee, cocoa-nuts, and a few cases of opium. The stowage was clumsily done, and the vessel consequently crank.

We got under way with a mere breath of wind, and for many days stood along the eastern coast of Java, without any other incident to beguile the monotony of our course than the occasional meeting with some of the small grabs of the Archipelago to which we were bound.

One evening, leaning over the taffrail, I observed a very singular, isolated cloud, to the N. W. It was remarkable, as well for its color, as from its being the first we had seen since our departure from Batavia. I watched it attentively until sunset, when it spread all at once to the eastward and westward, girting in the horizon with a narrow strip of vapor, and looking like a long line of low beach. My notice was soon afterwards attracted by the dusky-red appearance of the moon, and the peculiar character of the sea. The latter was undergoing a rapid change, and the water seemed more than usually transparent. Although I could distinctly see the bottom, yet heaving the lead, I found the ship in fifteen fathoms. The air now became intolerably hot, and was loaded with spiral exhalations similar to those arising from heated iron. As night came on, every breath of wind died away, and a more entire calm it is impossible to conceive. The flame of a candle burned upon the poop without the least perceptible motion, and a long hair, held between the finger and thumb, hung without the possibility of detecting a vibration. However, as the captain said he could perceive no indication of danger, and as we were drifting in bodily to shore, he ordered the sails to be furled, and the anchor let go. No watch was set, and the crew, consisting principally of Malays, stretched themselves deliberately upon deck. I went below—not without a full presentiment of evil. Indeed, every appearance warranted me in apprehending a simoom. I told the captain of my fears, but he paid no attention to what I said, and left me without deigning to give a reply. My uneasiness, however, prevented me from sleeping, and about midnight I went upon deck. —As I placed my foot upon the upper step of the companion-ladder, I was startled by a loud, humming noise, like that occasioned by the rapid revolution of a mill-wheel, and before I could ascertain its meaning, I found the ship quivering to its centre. In the next instant, a wilderness of foam hurled us upon our beam-ends, and, rushing over us fore and aft, swept the entire decks from stem to stern.

The extreme fury of the blast proved, in a great measure, the salvation of the ship. Although completely water-logged, yet, as her masts had gone by the board, she rose, after a minute, heavily from the sea, and, staggering awhile beneath the immense pressure of the tempest, finally righted.

By what miracle I escaped destruction, it is impossible to say. Stunned by the shock of the water, I found myself, upon recovery, jammed in between the stern-post and rudder. With great difficulty I gained my feet and looking dizzily around, was, at first, struck with the idea of our being among breakers so terrific, beyond the wildest imagination, was the whirlpool of mountainous and foaming ocean within which we were engulfed. After a while, I heard the voice of an old Swede, who had shipped with us at the moment of our leaving port. I hallooed to him with all my strength, and presently he came reeling aft. We soon discovered that we were the sole survivors of the accident. All on deck, with the exception of ourselves, had been swept overboard; —the captain and mates must have perished as they slept, for the cabins were deluged with water. Without assistance, we could expect to do little for the security of the ship, and our exertions were at first paralyzed by the momentary expectation of going down. Our cabin had, of course, parted like pack-thread, at the first breath of the hurricane, or we should have been instantaneously overwhelmed. We scudded with frightful velocity before the sea, and the water made clear breaches over us. The frame-work of our stern was shattered excessively, and, in almost every respect, we had received considerable injury; but to our extreme joy we found the pumps unchoked, and that we had made no great shifting of our ballast. The main fury of the blast had already blown over, and we apprehended little danger from the violence of the wind; but we looked forward to its total cessation with dismay; well believing, that in our shattered condition, we should inevitably perish in the tremendous swell which would ensue. But this very just apprehension seemed by no means likely to be soon verified. For five entire days and nights—during which our only subsistence was a small quantity of jaggeree, procured with great difficulty from the forecastle—the hulk flew at a rate defying computation, before rapidly succeeding flaws of wind, which, without equaling the first violence of the simoom, were still more terrific than any tempest I had before encountered. Our course for the first four days was, with trifling variations, S. E. and by S.; and we must have run down the coast of New Holland. —On the fifth day the cold became extreme, although the wind had hauled round a point more to the northward. —The sun arose with a sickly yellow lustre, and clambered a very few degrees above the horizon—emitting no decisive light. —There were no clouds apparent, yet the wind was upon the increase, and blew with a fitful and unsteady fury. About noon, as nearly as we could guess, our attention was again arrested by the appearance of the sun. It gave out no light, properly so called, but a dull and sullen glow without reflection, as if all its rays were polarized. Just before sinking within the turgid sea, its central fires suddenly went out, as if hurriedly extinguished by some unaccountable power. It was a dim, silver-like rim, alone, as it rushed down the unfathomable ocean.

We waited in vain for the arrival of the sixth day—that day to me has not arrived—to the Swede, never did arrive. Thence forward we were enshrouded in pitchy darkness, so that we could not have seen an object at twenty paces from the ship. Eternal night continued to envelop us, all unrelieved by the phosphoric sea-brilliancy to which we had been accustomed in the tropics. We observed too, that, although the tempest continued to rate with unabated violence, there was no longer to be discovered the usual appearance of surf, or foam, which had hitherto attended us. All around were horror, and thick gloom, and a black sweltering desert of ebony. —Superstitious terror crept by degrees into the spirit of the old Swede, and my own soul was wrapped up in silent wonder. We neglected all care of the ship, as worse than useless, and securing ourselves, as well as possible, to the stump of the mizen-mast, looked out bitterly into the world of ocean. We had no means of calculating time, nor could we form any guess of our situation. We were, however, well aware of having made farther to the southward than any previous navigators, and felt great amazement at not meeting with the usual impediments of ice. In the meantime every moment threatened to be our last—every mountainous billow hurried to overwhelm us. The swell surpassed anything I had imagined possible, and that we were not instantly buried is a miracle. My companion spoke of the lightness of our cargo, and reminded me of the excellent qualities of our ship; but I could not help feeling the utter hopelessness of hope itself, and prepared myself gloomily for that death which I thought nothing could defer beyond an hour, as, with every knot of way the ship made, the swelling of the black stupendous seas became more dismally appalling. At times we gasped for breath at an elevation beyond the albatross—at times became dizzy with the velocity of our descent into some watery hell, where the air grew stagnant, and no sound disturbed the slumbers of the kraken.

We were at the bottom of one of these abysses, when a quick scream from my companion broke fearfully upon the night. 'See! see!' cried he, shrieking in my ears, 'Almighty God! see! see!' As he spoke, I became aware of a dull, sullen glare of red light which streamed down the sides of the vast chasm where we lay, and threw a fitful brilliancy upon our deck. Casting my eyes upwards, I beheld a spectacle which froze the current of my blood. At a terrific height directly above us, and upon the very verge of the precipitous descent, hovered a gigantic ship of perhaps, four thousand tons. Although upreared upon the summit of a wave more than a hundred times her own altitude, her apparent size still exceeded that of any ship of the line or East Indiaman in existence. Her huge hull was a deep dingy black, unrelieved by any of the customary carvings of a ship. A single row of brass cannon protruded from her open ports, and dashed from their polished surfaces the fires of innumerable battle-lanterns, which swung to and fro about her rigging. But what mainly inspired us with horror and astonishment, was that she bore up under a press of sail in the very teeth of that supernatural sea, and of that ungovernable hurricane. When we first discovered her, her bows were alone to be seen, as she rose slowly from the dim and horrible gulf beyond her. For a moment of intense terror she paused upon the giddy pinnacle, as if in contemplation of her own sublimity, then trembled and tottered, and—came down.

At this instant, I know not what sudden self-possession came over my spirit. Staggering as far aft as I could, I awaited fearlessly the ruin that was to overwhelm. Our own vessel was at length ceasing from her struggles, and sinking with her head to the sea. The shock of the descending mass struck her, consequently, in that portion of her frame which was already under water, and the inevitable result was to hurl me, with irresistible violence, upon the rigging of the stranger.

As I fell, the ship hove in stays, and went about; and to the confusion ensuing I attributed my escape from the notice of the crew. With little difficulty I made my way unperceived to the main hatchway, which was partially open, and soon found an opportunity of secreting myself in the hold. Why I did so I can hardly tell. An indefinite sense of awe, which at first sight of the navigators of the ship had taken hold of my mind, was perhaps the principle of my concealment. I was unwilling to trust myself with a race of people who had offered, to the cursory glance I had taken, so many points of vague novelty, doubt, and apprehension. I therefore thought proper to contrive a hiding-place in the hold. This I did by removing a small portion of the shifting-boards, in such a manner as to afford me a convenient retreat between the huge timbers of the ship.

I had scarcely completed my work, when a footstep in the hold forced me to make use of it. A man passed by my place of concealment with a feeble and unsteady gait. I could not see his face, but had an opportunity of observing his general appearance. There was about it an evidence of great age and infirmity. His knees tottered beneath a load of years, and his entire frame quivered under the burthen. He muttered to himself, in a low broken tone, some words of a language which I could not understand, and groped in a corner among a pile of singular-looking instruments, and decayed charts of navigation. His manner was a wild mixture of the peevishness of second childhood, and the solemn dignity of a God. He at length went on deck, and I saw him no more.

o   o   o

A feeling, for which I have no name, has taken possession of my soul—a sensation which will admit of no analysis, to which the lessons of by-gone times are inadequate, and for which I fear futurity itself will offer me no key. To a mind constituted like my own, the latter consideration is an evil. I shall never—I know that I shall never—be satisfied with regard to the nature of my conceptions. Yet it is not wonderful that these conceptions are indefinite, since they have their origin in sources so utterly novel. A new sense— a new entity is added to my soul.

o o o

It is long since I first trod the deck of this terrible ship, and the rays of my destiny are, I think, gathering to a focus. Incomprehensible men! Wrapped up in meditations of a kind which I cannot divine, they pass me by unnoticed. Concealment is utter folly on my part, for the people will not see. It was but just now that I passed directly before the eyes of the mate—it was no long while ago that I ventured into the captain's own private cabin, and took thence the materials with which I write, and have written. I shall from time to time continue this journal. It is true that I may not find an opportunity of transmitting it to the world, but I will not fail to make the endeavour. At the last moment I will enclose the MS. in a bottle, and cast it within the sea.

o o o

An incident has occurred which has given me new room for meditation. Are such things the operation of ungoverned Chance? I had ventured upon deck and thrown myself down, without attracting any notice, among a pile of ratlin-stuff and old sails, in the bottom of the yawl. While musing upon the singularity of my fate, I unwittingly daubed with a tar-brush the edges of a neatly folded studding-sail which lay near me on a barrel. The studding-sail is now bent upon the ship, and the thoughtless touches of the brush are spread out into the word DISCOVERY.

I have made many observations lately upon the structure of the vessel. Although well armed, she is not, I think, a ship of war. Her rigging, build, and general equipment, all negative a supposition of this kind. What she is not, I can easily perceive—what she *is not*, I can easily perceive—what she *is* I fear it is impossible to say. I know not how it is, but in scrutinizing her strange model and singular cast of spars, her huge size and overgrown suits of canvas, her severely simple bow and antiquated stern, there will occasionally flash across my mind a sensation of familiar things, and there is always mixed up with such indistinct shadows of recollection, an unaccountable memory of old foreign chronicles and ages long ago.

I have been looking at the timbers of the ship. She is built of a material to which I am a stranger. There is a peculiar character about the wood which strikes me as rendering it unfit for the purpose to which it has been applied. I mean its extreme *porousness,* considered independently of the worm-eaten condition which is a consequence of navigation in these seas, and apart from the rottenness attendant upon age. It will appear perhaps an observation somewhat over-curious, but this wood would have every characteristic of Spanish oak, if Spanish oak were distended by any unnatural means.

In reading the above sentence a curious apothegm of an old weather-beaten Dutch navigator comes full upon my recollection. 'It is as sure,' he was wont to say, when any doubt was entertained of his veracity, 'as sure as there is a sea where the ship itself will grow in bulk like the living body of the seaman.'

About an hour ago, I made bold to thrust myself among a group of the crew. They paid me no manner of attention, and although I stood in the very midst of them all, seemed utterly unconscious of my presence. Like the one I had at first seen in the hold, they all bore about them the marks of a hoary old age. Their knees trembled with infirmity; their shoulders were bent double with decrepitude; their shrivelled skins rattled in the wind; their voices were low, tremulous and broken; their eyes glistened with the rheum of years; and their gray hairs streamed terribly in the tempest. Around them, on every part of the deck, lay scattered mathematical instruments of the most quaint and obsolete construction.

I mentioned some time ago the bending of a studding-sail. From that period the ship, being thrown dead off the wind, has continued her terrific course due south, with every rag of canvas packed upon her, from her trucks to her lower studding-sail booms, and rolling every moment her top-gallant yard-arms into the most appalling hell of water which it can enter into the mind of man to imagine. I have just left the deck, where I find it impossible to maintain a footing, although the crew seem to experience little inconvenience. It appears to me a miracle of miracles that our enormous bulk is not swallowed up at once and forever. We are surely doomed to hover continually upon the brink of Eternity, without taking a final plunge into the abyss. From billows a thousand times more stupendous than any I have ever seen, we glide away with the facility of the arrowy sea-gull; and the colossal waters rear their heads above us like demons of the deep, but like demons confined to simple threats and forbidden to destroy. I am led to attribute these frequent escapes to the only natural cause which can account for such effect. —I must suppose the ship to be within the influence of some strong current, or impetuous under-tow.

I have seen the captain face to face, and in his own cabin—but, as I expected, he paid me no attention. Although in his appearance there is, to a casual observer, nothing which might bespeak him more or less than man—still a feeling of irrepressible reverence and awe mingled with the sensation of wonder with which I regarded him. In stature he is nearly my own height; that is, about five feet eight inches. He is of a well-knit and compact frame of body, neither robust nor remarkable otherwise. But it is the singularity of the expression which reigns upon the face—it is the intense, the wonderful, the thrilling evidence of old age, so utter, so extreme, which excites within my spirit a sense—a sentiment ineffable. His forehead, although little wrinkled, seems to bear upon it the stamp of a myriad of years.—His gray hairs are records of the past, and his grayer eyes are Sybils of the future. The cabin floor was thickly strewn with strange, iron-clasped folios, and mouldering instruments of science, and obsolete long-forgotten charts. His head was bowed down upon his hands, and he pored, with a fiery unquiet eye, over a paper which I took to be a commission, and which, at all events, bore the signature of a monarch. He muttered to himself, as did the first seaman whom I saw in the hold, some low peevish syllables of a foreign tongue, and although the speaker was close at my elbow, his voice seemed to reach my ears from the distance of a mile.

The ship and all in it are imbued with the spirit of Eld. The crew glide to and fro, like the ghosts of buried centuries their eyes have an eager and uneasy meaning; and when their fingers fall athwart my path in the wild glare of the battle-lanterns, I feel as I have never felt before, although I have been all my life a dealer in antiquities, and have imbibed the shadows of fallen columns at Balbec, and Tadmore, and Persepolis, until my very soul has become a ruin.

When I look around me I feel ashamed of my former apprehensions. If I trembled at the blast which has hitherto attended us, shall I not stand aghast at a warring of wind and ocean, to convey any idea of which the words *tornado* and *simoom* are trivial and ineffective? All in the immediate vicinity of the ship is the blackness of eternal night, and a chaos of foamless water; but, about a league on either side of us, may be seen, indistinctly and at intervals, stupendous ramparts of ice, towering away into the desolate sky, and looking like the walls of the universe.

As I imagined, the ship proves to be in a current; if that appellation can properly be given to a tide which, howling and shrieking by the white ice, thunders on to the southward with a velocity like the headlong dashing of a cataract.

To conceive the horror of my sensations is, I presume, utterly impossible; yet a curiosity to penetrate the mysteries of these awful regions, predominates even over my despair, and will reconcile me to the most hideous aspect of death. It is evident that we are hurrying onwards to some exciting knowledge—some never-to-be-imparted secret, whose attainment is destruction. Perhaps this current leads us to the southern pole itself. It must be confessed that a supposition apparently so wild has every probability in its favor.

The crew pace the deck with unquiet and tremulous step; but there is upon their countenances an expression more of the eagerness of hope than of the apathy of despair.

In the meantime the wind is still in our poop, and, as we carry a crowd of canvas, the ship is at times lifted bodily from out the sea—Oh, horror upon horror! the ice opens suddenly to the right, and to the left, and we are whirling dizzily, in immense concentric circles, round and round the borders of a gigantic amphitheatre, the summit of whose walls is lost in the darkness and the distance. But little time will be left me to ponder upon my destiny—the circles rapidly grow small—we are plunging madly within the grasp of the whirlpool—and amid a roaring, and bellowing, and thundering of ocean and of tempest, the ship is quivering, oh God! and—going down.

FROM *THE PERFECT STORM*
SEBASTIAN *JUNGER*

In October 1991 a hellish, unnamed hurricane took the lives of the crew of a swordfishing boat off the North Atlantic coast. In The Perfect Storm, *Sebastian Junger reconstructs the last voyage of the* Andrea Gail.

For reasons that he still doesn't understand, Hazard didn't quit. He made a guess and swam. The entire port side of the cabin was welded steel and he knew if he picked that direction, he was finished. He felt himself slide through a narrow opening—the door? a window? —and suddenly he was back in the world. The boat was hull-up, sliding away fast, and the life raft was convulsing at the end of its tether. It was his only hope; he wriggled out of his clothes and started to swim.

Whether the *Andrea Gail* rolls, pitch-poles, or gets driven down, she winds up, one way or another, in a position from which she cannot recover. Among marine architects this is known as the zero-moment point—the point of no return. The transition from crisis to catastrophe is fast, probably under a minute, or someone would've tripped the EPIRB [Emergency Position Indicating Radio Beacon]. (In fact the EPIRB doesn't even signal when it hits the water, which means it has somehow malfunctioned. In the vast majority of cases, the Coast Guard knows when men are dying offshore.) There's no time to put on survival suits or grab a life vest; the boat's moving through the most extreme motion of her life and there isn't even time to shout. The refrigerator comes out of the wall and crashes across the gallery. Dirty dishes cascade out of the sink. The TV, the washing machine, the VCR tapes, the men, all go flying. And, seconds later, the water moves in.

When a boat floods, the first thing that happens is that her electrical system shorts out. The lights go off, and for a few moments the only illumination is the frenetic blue of sparks arching down into the water. It's said that people in extreme situations perceive things in distorted, almost surreal ways, and when the wires start to crackle and burn, perhaps one of the crew thinks of fireworks—of the last Fourth of July, walking around Gloucester with his girlfriend and watching colors blossom over the inner harbor. There'd be tourists shuffling down Rogers Street and fishermen hooting from bars and the smell of gunpowder and fried clams drifting through town. He'd have his whole life ahead of him, that July evening; he'd have every choice in the world.

And he wound up swordfishing. He wound up, by one route or another, on this trip, in this storm, with this boat filling up with water and one or two minutes left to live. There's no going back now, no rescue helicopter that could possibly save him. All that's left is to hope it's over fast.

When the water first hits the trapped men, it's cold but not paralyzing, around fifty-two degrees. A man can survive up to four hours in that temperature if something holds him up. If the boat rolls or flips over, the men in the wheelhouse are the first to drown. Their experience is exactly like Hazard's except that they don't make it out of the wheelhouse to a life raft; they inhale and that's it. After that the water rises up the companionway, flooding the galley and berths, and then starts up the inverted engine room hatch. It may well be pouring in the aft door and the fish hatch, too, if either failed during the sinking. If the boat is hull-up and there are men in the engine room, they are the last to die. They're in absolute darkness, under a landslide of tools and gear, the water rising up the companionway and the roar of the waves probably very muted through the hull. If the water takes long enough, they might attempt to escape on a lungful of air—down the companionway, along the hall, through the aft door and out from under the boat—but they don't make it. It's too far, they die trying. Or the water comes up so hard and fast that they can't even think. They're up to their waists and then their chests and then their chins and then there's no air at all. Just what's in their lungs, a minute's worth or so.

The instinct not to breathe underwater is so strong that it overcomes the agony of running out of air. No matter how desperate the drowning person is, he doesn't inhale until he's on the verge of losing consciousness. At that point there's so much carbon dioxide in the blood, and so little oxygen, that chemical sensors in the brain trigger an involuntary breath whether he's underwater or not. That is called the "break point"; laboratory experiments have shown the break point to come after eighty-seven seconds. It's a sort of neurological optimism, as if the body were saying, *Holding our breath is killing us, and breathing in might not kill us, so we might as well breathe in.* If the person hyperventilates first——as free divers do, and as a frantic person might—the break point comes as late as 140 seconds. Hyperventilation initially flushes carbon dioxide out of the system, so it takes that much longer to climb back up to critical levels.

Until the break point, a drowning person is said to be undergoing "voluntary apnea," choosing not to breathe. Lack of oxygen to the brain causes a sensation of darkness closing in from all sides, as in a camera aperture stopping down. The panic of a drowning person is mixed with an odd incredulity that this is actually happening. Having never done it before, the body—and the mind—do not know how to die gracefully. The process is filled with desperation and awkwardness. "So *this* is drowning," a drowning person might think. "So *this* is how my life finally ends."

Along with the disbelief is an overwhelming sense of being wrenched from life at the most banal, inopportune moment imaginable. "I can't die, I have tickets to next week's game," is not an impossible thought for someone who is drowning. The drowning person may even feel embarrassed, as if he's squandered a great fortune. He has an image of people shaking their heads over his dying so senselessly. The drowning person may feel as if it's the last, greatest act of stupidity in his life.

These thoughts shriek through the mind during the minute or so that it takes a panicked person to run out of air. When the first involuntary breath occurs most people are still conscious, which is unfortunate, because the only thing more unpleasant than running out of air is breathing in water. At that point the person goes from voluntary to involuntary apnea, and the drowning begins in earnest. A spasmodic breath drags water into the mouth and windpipe, and then one of two things happen. In about ten percent of people, water—anything—touching the vocal cords triggers an immediate contraction in the muscles around the larynx. In effect, the central nervous system judges something in the voice box to be more of a threat than low oxygen levels in the blood, and acts accordingly. This is called a laryngo-spasm. It's so powerful that it overcomes the breathing reflex and eventually suffocates the person. A person with laryngospasm drowns without any water in his lungs.

In the other ninety percent of people, water floods the lungs and ends any waning transfer of oxygen to the blood. The clock is running down now; half-conscious and enfeebled by oxygen depletion, the person is in no position to fight his way back up to the surface. The very process of drowning makes it harder and harder not to drown, an exponential disaster curve similar to that of a sinking boat.

Occasionally someone makes it back from this dark world, though, and it's from these people that we know what drowning feels like. In 1892, a Scottish doctor named

James Lowson was on a steamship bound for Colombo, Sri Lanka, when they ran into a typhoon and went down in the dead of night. Most of the 150 people on board sank with the ship, but Lowson managed to fight his way out of the hold and over the side. The ship sank out from under his feet, dragging him down, and the last thing he remembers is losing consciousness underwater. A few minutes later the buoyancy of his life vest shot him to the surface, though, and he washed up on an island and lived to write about his experiences in the *Edinburgh Medical Journal*. He attributed the clarity of his recollection to the "preternatural calm" of people facing death. It's as close as one is going to get to the last moments of the *Andrea Gail*:

> All afternoon the hammering of the big seas on the doomed vessel went on, whilst night came only to add darkness to our other horrors. Shortly before ten o'clock three tremendous seas found their way down the stokehole, putting out the fires, and our situation was desperate. The end came shortly before midnight, when there was a heavy crash on the reef, and the vessel was lying at the bottom of the Straits of Formosa in under a minute.

> With scarcely time to think I pulled down the lifebelts and, throwing two to my companions, tied the third on myself and bolted for the companionway. There was no time to spare for studying humanity at this juncture, but I can never forget the apparent want of initiative in all I passed. All the passengers seemed paralyzed—

even my companions, some of them able military men. The stewards of the ship, uttering cries of despair and last farewells, blocked the entrance to the deck, and it was only by sheer force I was able to squeeze past them. Getting out on deck, a perfect mountain of water seemed to come from overhead, as well as from below, and dashed me against the bridge companion-way. The ship was going down rapidly, and I was pulled down with her, struggling to extricate myself.

I got clear under water and immediately struck out to reach the surface, only to go farther down. This exertion was a serious waste of breath, and after ten or fifteen seconds the effort of inspiration could no longer be restrained. It seemed as if I was in a vice which was gradually being screwed up tight until it felt as if the sternum and spinal column must break. Many years ago my old teacher used to describe how painless and easy a death by drowning was—"like falling about in a green field in early summer"—and this flashed across my brain at the time. The "gulping" efforts became less frequent, and the pressure seemed unbearable, but gradually the pain seemed to ease up. I appeared to be in a pleasant dream, although I had enough will power to think of friends at home and the sight of the Grampians, familiar to me as a boy, that was brought into my view. Before losing consciousness the chest pain had completely disappeared and the sensation was actually pleasant.

When consciousness returned, I found myself at the surface, and managed to get a dozen good inspirations. Land was about four hundred yards distant, and I used a bale of silk and then a long wooden plank to assist me to shore. On landing, and getting behind a sheltering rock, no effort was required to produce copius emesis. After the excitement, sound sleep set in, and this sleep lasted three hours, when a profuse diarrhea came on, evidently brought on by the sea water ingested. Until morning broke all my muscles were in a constant tremor which could not be controlled. (Several weeks later) I was sleeping in a comfortable bed and, late in the evening, a nightmare led to my having a severe struggle with the bedroom furniture, finally taking a "header" out of the bed and coming to grief on the floor.

Lowson guesses that laryngospasm prevented water from entering his lungs when he was unconscious. The crew of the *Andrea Gail* either have laryngospasms or completely inundated lungs. They are suspended, open-eyed and unconscious, in the flooded enclosures of the boat. The darkness is absolute and the boat may already be on her way to the bottom. At this point only a massive amount of oxygen could save these men. They have suffered, at most, a minute or two. Their bodies, having imposed increasingly drastic measures to keep functioning, have finally started to shut down. Water in the lungs washes away a substance called surfactant, which enables the alveoli to leach oxygen out of the air. The alveoli themselves, grape-like clusters of membrane on the lung wall, collapse because blood cannot get through the pulmonary artery. The artery has constricted in an effort to shunt blood to areas of the lungs where there is more oxygen. Unfortunately, those don't exist. The heart labors under critically low levels of oxygen and starts to beat erratically—"like a bag full of worms," as one doctor says. This is called ventricular fibrillation. The more irregularly the heart beats, the less blood it moves and the faster life functions decline. Children—who have proportionally stronger hearts than adults—can maintain a heartbeat for up to five minutes without air. Adults die faster. The heart beats less and less effectively until, after several minutes, there's no movement at all. Only the brain is alive.

The central nervous system does not know what has happened to the body; all it knows is that not enough oxygen is getting to the brain. Orders are still being issued—*Breathe! Pump! Circulate!*—that the body cannot obey. If the person were defibrillated at that moment, he might possibly survive. He could be given cardiopulmonary resuscitation, put on a respirator, and coaxed back to life. Still, the body is doing everything it can to delay the inevitable. When cold water touches the face, an impulse travels along the trigeminal and vagus nerves to the central nervous system and lowers the metabolic rate. The pulse slows down and the blood pools where it's needed most, in the heart and skull. It's a sort of temporary hibernation that drastically reduces the body's need for oxygen. Nurses will splash ice water on the face of a person with a racing heart to trigger the same reaction.

The diving reflex, as this is called, is compounded by the general effect of cold temperature on tissue—it preserves it. All chemical reactions, and metabolic processes, become honey-slow, and the brain can get by on less than half the oxygen it normally requires. There are cases of people spending forty or fifty minutes under lake ice and surviving. The colder the water, the stronger the diving reflex, the slower the metabolic processes, and the longer the survival time. The crew of the *Andrea Gail* do not find themselves in particularly cold water, though; it may add five or ten minutes to their lives. And there is no one around to save them anyway. The electrical activity in their brain gets weaker and weaker until, after fifteen or twenty minutes, it ceases altogether.

The body could be likened to a crew that resorts to increasingly desperate measures to keep their vessel afloat. Eventually the last wire has shorted out, the last bit of decking has settled under the water. Tyne, Pierre, Sullivan, Moran, Murphy, and Shatford are dead.

FROM *TYPHOON*

JOSEPH CONRAD

Jukes was as ready a man as any half-dozen young mates that may be caught by casting a net upon the waters; and though he had been somewhat taken aback by the startling viciousness of the first squall, he had pulled himself together on the instant, had called out the hands and had rushed them along to secure such openings about the deck as had not been already battened down earlier in the evening. Shouting in his fresh, stentorian voice, "Jump, boys, and bear a hand!" he led in the work, telling himself the while that he had "just expected this."

But at the same time he was growing aware that this was rather more than he had expected. From the first stir of the air felt on his cheek the gale seemed to take upon itself the accumulated impetus of an avalanche. Heavy sprays enveloped the *Nan-Shan* from stem to stern, and instantly in the midst of her regular rolling she began to jerk and plunge as though she had gone mad with fright.

Jukes thought, "This is not joke." While he was exchanging explanatory yells with his captain, a sudden lowering of the darkness came upon the night, falling before their vision like something palpable. It was as if the masked lights of the world had been turned down. Jukes was uncritically glad to have his captain at hand. It relieved him as though that man had, by simply coming on deck, taken most of the gale's weight upon his shoulders. Such is the prestige, the privilege, and the burden of command.

Captain MacWhirr could expect no relief of that sort from anyone on earth. Such is the loneliness of command. He was trying to see, with that watchful manner of a seaman who stares into the wind's eye as if into the eye of an adversary, to penetrate the hidden intention and guess the aim and force of the thrust. The strong wind swept at him out of a vast obscurity; he felt under his feet the uneasiness of his ship, and he could not even discern the shadow of her shape. He wished it were not so; and very still he waited, feeling stricken by a blind man's helplessness.

To be silent was natural to him, dark or shine. Jukes, at his elbow, made himself heard yelling cheerily in the gusts, "We must have got the worst of it at once, sir." A faint burst of lightning quivered all round, as if flashed into a cavern—into a black and secret chamber of the sea, with a floor of foaming crests.

It unveiled for a sinister, fluttering moment a ragged mass of clouds hanging low, the lurch of the long outlines of the ship, the black figures of men caught on the bridge, heads forward, as if petrified in the act of butting. The darkness palpitated down upon all this, and then the real thing came at last.

It was something formidable and swift, like the sudden smashing of a vial of wrath. It seemed to explode all round the ship with an overpowering concussion and a rush of great waters, as if an immense dam had been blown up to windward. In an instant the men lost touch of each other. This is the disintegrating power of a great wind: it isolates one from one's kind. An earthquake, a landslip, an avalanche, overtake a man incidentally, as it were—without passion. A furious gale attacks him like a personal enemy, tries to grasp his limbs, fastens upon his mind, seeks to rout his very spirit out of him.

Jukes was driven away from his commander. He fancied himself whirled a great distance through the air. Everything disappeared—even, for a moment, his power of thinking; but his hand had found one of the rail stanchions. His distress was by no means alleviated by an inclination to disbelieve the reality of this experience. Though young, he had seen some bad weather, and had never doubted his ability to imagine the worst; but this was so much beyond his powers of fancy that it appeared incompatible with the existence of any ship whatever. He would have been incredulous about himself in the same way, perhaps, had he not been so harassed by the necessity of exerting a wrestling effort against a force trying to tear him away from his hold. Moreover, the conviction of not being utterly destroyed returned to him through the sensations of being half-drowned, bestially shaken, and partly choked.

It seemed to him he remained there precariously alone with the stanchion for a long, long time. The rain poured on him, flowed, drove in sheets. He breathed in gasps; and sometimes the water he swallowed was fresh and sometimes it was salt. For the most part he kept his eyes shut tight, as if suspecting his sight might be destroyed in the immense flurry of the elements. When he ventured to blink hastily, he derived some moral support from the green gleam of the starboard light shining feebly upon the flight of rain and sprays. He was actually looking at it when its ray fell upon the uprearing sea which put it out. He saw the head of the wave topple over, adding the mite of its crash to the tremendous uproar raging around him, and almost at the same instant the stanchion was wrenched away from his embracing arms. After a crushing thump on his back he found himself suddenly afloat and borne upwards. His first irresistible notion was that the whole China Sea had climbed on the bridge. Then, more sanely, he concluded himself gone overboard. All the time he was being tossed, flung, and rolled in great volumes of water, he kept on repeating mentally, with the utmost precipitation, the words: "My God! My God! My God! My God!"

All at once, in a revolt of misery and despair, he formed the crazy resolution to get out of that. And he began to thrash about with his arms and legs. But as soon as he commenced his wretched struggles he discovered that he had become somehow mixed up with a face, an oilskin coat, somebody's boots. He clawed ferociously all these things in turn, lost them, found them again, lost them once more, and finally was himself caught in the firm clasp of a pair of stout arms. He returned the embrace closely round a thick solid body. He had found his captain.

They tumbled over and over, tightening their hug. Suddenly the water let them down with a brutal bang; and, stranded against the side of the wheelhouse, out of breath and bruised, they were left to stagger up in the wind and hold on where they could.

Jukes came out of it rather horrified, as though he had escaped some unparalleled outrage directed at his feelings. It weakened his faith in himself. He started shouting aimlessly to the man he could feel near him in that fiendish blackness, "Is it you sir? Is it you sir?" till his temples seemed ready to burst. And he heard in answer a voice, as if crying far away, as if screaming to him fretfully from a very great distance, the one word "Yes!" Other seas swept again over the bridge. He received them defenselessly right over his bare head, with both his hands engaged in holding.

The motion of the ship was extravagant. Her lurches had an appalling helplessness: she pitched as if taking a header into a void, and seemed to find a wall to hit every time. When she rolled she fell on her side headlong, and she would be righted back by such a demolishing blow that Jukes felt her reeling as a clubbed man reels before he collapses. The gale howled and scuffled about gigantically in the darkness, as though the entire world were one black gully. At certain moments the air streamed against the ship as if sucked through a tunnel with a concentrated solid force of impact that seemed to lift her clean out of the water and keep her up for an instant with only a quiver running through her from end to end. And then she would begin her tumbling again as if dropped back into a boiling caldron. Jukes tried hard to compose his mind and judge things coolly.

The sea, flattened down in the heavier gusts, would uprise and overwhelm both ends of the *Nan-Shan* in snowy rushes of foam, expanding wide, beyond both rails, into the night. And on this dazzling sheet, spread under the blackness of the clouds and emitting a bluish glow, Captain MacWhirr could catch a desolate glimpse of a few tiny specks black as ebony, the tops of the hatches, the battened companions, the heads of the covered winches, the foot of a mast. This was all he could see of his ship. Her middle structure, covered by the bridge which bore him, his mate, the closed wheelhouse where a man was steering shut up with the fear of being swept overboard together with the whole thing in one great crash—her middle structure was like a half-tide rock awash upon a coast. It was like an outlying rock with the water boiling up, streaming over, pouring off, beating round—like a rock in the surf to which shipwrecked people cling before they let go—only it rose, it sank, it rolled continuously, without respite and rest, like a rock that should have miraculously struck adrift from a coast and gone wallowing upon the sea.

The *Nan-San* was being looted by the storm with a senseless, destructive fury: trysails torn out of the extra gaskets, double-lashed awnings blown away, bridge swept clean, weather cloths burst, rails twisted, light-screens smashed—and two of the boats had gone already. They had gone unheard and unseen, melting, as it were, in the shock and smother of the wave. It was only later, when upon the white flash of another high sea hurling itself amidships, Jukes had a vision of two pairs of davits leaping black and empty out of the solid blackness, with one overhauled fall flying and an ironbound block capering in the air, that he became aware of what had happened within about three yards of his back.

He poked his head forward, groping for the ear of his commander. His lips touched it—big, fleshy, very wet. He cried in an agitated tone, "Our boats are going now, sir."

And again he heard that voice, forced and ringing feebly, but with a penetrating effect of quietness in the enormous discord of noises, as if sent out from some remote spot of peace beyond the black wastes of the gale; again he heard a man's voice—the frail and indomitable sound that can be made to carry an infinity of thought, resolution and purpose, that shall be pronouncing confident words on the last day, when heavens fall, and justice is done—again he heard it, and it was crying to him, as if from very, very far—"All right."

He thought he had not managed to make himself understood. "Our boats—I say boats—the boats, sir! Two gone!"

The same voice, within a foot of him and yet so remote, yelled sensibly, "Can't be helped."

Captain MacWhirr had never turned his face, but Jukes caught some more words on the wind.

"What can—expect—when hammering through—such—Bound to leave—something behind—stands to reason."

Watchfully Jukes listened for more. No more came. This was all Captain MacWhirr had to say; and Jukes could picture to himself rather than see the broad squat back before him. An impenetrable obscurity pressed down upon the ghostly glimmers of the sea. A dull conviction seized upon Jukes that there was nothing to be done.

If the steering gear did not give way, if the immense volumes of water did not burst the deck in or smash one of the hatches, if the engines did not give up, if way could be kept on the ship against this terrific wind, and she did not bury herself in one of these awful seas, of whose white crests alone, topping high above her bows, he could now and then get a sickening glimpse—then there was a chance of her coming out of it. Something within him seemed to turn over, bringing uppermost the feeling that the *Nan-Shan* was lost.

"She's done for," he said to himself, with a surprising mental agitation, as though he had discovered an unexpected meaning in this thought. One of these things was bound to happen. Nothing could be prevented now, and nothing could be remedied. The men on board did not count, and the ship could not last. This weather was too impossible.

Jukes felt an arm thrown heavily over his shoulders; and to this overture he responded with great intelligence by catching hold of his captain round the waist.

They stood clasped thus in the blind night, bracing each other against the wind, cheek to cheek and lip to ear, in the manner of two hulks lashed stem to stern together.

And Jukes heard the voice of his commander hardly any louder than before, but nearer, as though, starting to march athwart the prodigious rush of the hurricane, it had approached him, bearing that strange effect of quietness like the serene glow of a halo.

"D'ye know where the hands go to?" it asked, vigorous and evanescent at the same time, overcoming the strength of the wind, and swept away from Jukes instantly.

Jukes didn't know. They were all on the bridge when the real force of the hurricane struck the ship. He had no idea where they had crawled to. Under the circumstances they were nowhere, for all the use that could be made of them. Somehow the Captain's wish to know distressed Jukes.

"Want the hands, sir?" he cried, apprehensively.

"Ought to know," asserted Captain MacWhirr. "Hold hard."

They held hard. An outburst of unchained fury, a vicious rush of the wind absolutely steadied the ship; she rocked only, quick and light like a child's cradle, for a terrific moment of suspense, while the whole atmosphere, as it seemed, streamed furiously past her, roaring away from the tenebrous earth.

It suffocated them, and with eyes shut they tightened their grasp. What from the magnitude of the shock might have been a column of water running upright in the dark, butted against the ship, broke short, and fell on her bridge, crushingly, from on high, with a dead burying weight.

A flying fragment of that collapse, a mere splash, enveloped them in one swirl from their feet over their heads, filling violently their ears, mouths and nostrils with salt water. It knocked out their legs, wrenched in haste at their arms, seethed away swiftly under their chins; and opening their eyes, they saw the piled-up masses of foam dashing to and fro amongst what looked like the fragments of a ship. She had given way as if driven straight in. Their panting hearts yielded, too, before the tremendous blow; and all at once she sprang up again to her desperate plunging, as if trying to scramble out from under the ruins.

The seas in the dark seemed to rush from all sides to keep her back where she might perish. There was hate in the way she was handled, and a ferocity in the blows that fell. She was like a living creature thrown to the rage of a mob: hustled terribly, struck at, borne up, flung down, leaped upon. Captain MacWhirr and Jukes kept hold of each other, deafened by the noise, gagged by the wind; and the great physical tumult beating about their bodies, brought, like an unbridled display of passion, a profound trouble to their souls. One of those wild and appalling shrieks that are heard at times passing mysteriously overhead in the steady roar of a hurricane, swooped, as if borne on wings, upon the ship, and Jukes tried to outscream it.

"Will she live through this?"

The cry was wrenched out of his breast. It was as unintentional as the birth of a thought in the head, and he heard nothing of it himself. It all became extinct at once—thought, intention, effort—and of his cry the inaudible vibration added to the tempest waves of the air.

He expected nothing from it. Nothing at all. For indeed what answer could be made? But after a while he heard with amazement the frail and resisting voice in his ear, the dwarf sound, unconquered in the giant tumult.

"She may!"

It was a dull yell, more difficult to seize than a whisper. And presently the voice returned again, half submerged in the vast crashes, like a ship battling against the waves of an ocean.

"Let's hope so!" it cried—small, lonely and unmoved, a stranger to the visions of hope or fear; and it flickered into disconnected words: "Ship . . . This . . . Never—Anyhow . . . for the best." Jukes gave it up.

Then, as if it had come suddenly upon the one thing fit to withstand the power of a storm, it seemed to gain force and firmness for the last broken shouts:

"Keep on hammering . . . builders . . . good men. . . . And chance it . . . engines. . . . Rout . . . good man."

Captain MacWhirr removed his arm from Jukes' shoulders, and thereby ceased to exist for his mate, so dark it was; Jukes, after a tense stiffening of every muscle, would let himself go limp all over. The gnawing of profound discomfort existed side by side with an incredible disposition to somnolence, as though he had been buffeted and worried into drowsiness. The wind would get hold of his head and try to shake it off his shoulders; his clothes, full of water, were as heavy as lead, cold and dripping like an armor of melting ice: he shivered—it lasted a long time; and with his hands closed hard on his hold, he was letting himself sink slowly into the depths of bodily misery. His mind became concentrated upon himself in an aimless, idle way, and when something pushed lightly at the back of his knees he nearly, as the saying is, jumped out of his skin.

In the start forward he bumped the back of Captain MacWhirr, who didn't move; and then a hand gripped his thigh. A lull had come, a menacing lull of the wind, the holding of a stormy breath—and he felt himself pawed all over. It was the boatswain. Jukes recognized these hands, so thick and enormous that they seemed to belong to some new species of man.

The boatswain had arrived on the bridge, crawling on all fours against the wind, and had found the chief mate's legs with the top of his head. Immediately he crouched and began to explore Jukes' person upwards with prudent, apologetic touches, as became an inferior.

He was an ill-favored, undersized, gruff sailor of fifty, coarsely hairy, short-legged, long-armed, resembling an elderly ape. His strength was immense; and in his great lumpy paws, bulging like brown boxing gloves on the end of furry forearms, the heaviest objects were handled like playthings. Apart from the grizzled pelt on his chest, the menacing demeanor and the hoarse voice, he had none of the classical attributes of his rating. His good nature almost amounted to imbecility: the men did what they liked with him, and he had not an ounce of initiative in his character, which was easygoing and talkative. For these reasons Jukes disliked him; but Captain MacWhirr, to Jukes' scornful disgust, seemed to regard him as a first-rate petty officer.

He pulled himself up by Jukes' coat, taking that liberty with the greatest moderation, and only so far as it was forced upon him by the hurricane.

"What is it, bosun, what is it?" yelled Jukes, impatiently. What could that fraud of a bosun want on the bridge? The typhoon had got on Jukes' nerves. The husky bellowings of the other, though unintelligible, seemed to suggest a state of lively satisfaction. There could be no mistake. The old fool was pleased with something.

The boatswain's other hand had found some other body, for in a changed tone he began to inquire: "Is it you, sir? Is it you, sir?" The wind strangled his howls.

"Yes!" cried Captain MacWhirr.

IN A FOG
GEOFFREY **WOLFF**

The full moon lit Boston shortly before midnight. Precisely:
The moon edged over the horizon at 11:27 that eleventh
day of July, as good as my pledge to my wife and two sons.
I had warranted much, that we'd have fun, for example.
The notion was definitely to have a good time. That was
always the idea, to take pleasure from doing something
just so, from coming through in the crunch (if, God forbid,
there should be a crunch), and caring for the boat and your
loved ones. Priscilla, Justin, Nicholas, and I had embarked
on a routine cruising adventure, a voyage Down East: Nar-
ragansett Bay to Cuttyhunk, Massachusetts; Cuttyhunk
to Wings Neck; through the Cape Cod Canal to Race Point
buoy off Provincetown; thence a straight shot offshore, 120
very nautical miles northeast to Monhegan Island, its light
visible twenty miles, or so I believed.

Now, just past midnight, we were gurgling down-
wind across Massachusetts Bay; Nicholas, at the helm,

showed me the Big Dipper up there. Seas were moderate, as promised, slapping reassuringly against the counter of *Blackwing*, our Mystic 30 cutter. Hazy, hot afternoon in Cape Cod Bay as advertised, wind sou'west, just what the weatherman had said.

That warm night in the cockpit, aboard a boat I love, with the three people I most care about, doing a thing I cannot get enough of doing, bound for Casco and Penobscot bays, watching my fourteen-year-old boy anticipate the shove of a swell and correct for it, watching him scan the horizon for ships lucky enough to be in the neighborhood that gorgeous night, well, wasn't this as good as it got? Wasn't this, in fact, my *doing?*

Of all provocations for my smugness that soft night, the most urgent was the appearance, precisely when and where it was meant to rise, of the moon's sharp-edged silver face, like a cheerful, goofy neighbor peering over a fence. *Hey, Guys, what's cookin'?* Eldridge had said it would be so and it was so, benign prophecy, the spheres in their regulated cycles, time and tide, all right with the world, natural law at the helm (and steering sure).

Justin was below, sleeping an eleven-year-old's serious sleep, and Priscilla slept, too. And this was good: They trusted me. I'd said how it would be and it had been that and more. Late afternoon, a couple of hours after leaving Race Point, offsoundings, we had sailed into a pod of humpbacks. I hadn't promised whales, but I'd delivered whales. Now we were talking of them, how they'd simply materialized, not there and then there. We talked about their show-off explosion of water breaching, great theater, a big-scale memory for us.

Now Nick was talking about things more comfortably discussed in the dark, away from home. A girlfriend from sixth grade. Fears and disappointments. Bewilderments. My son was backlit by the moon, and the sea was most remarkable pewter. We talked about the Bomb, ghosts, What's the Meaning of Life.

And then I was tired. Suddenly and bone-achingly tapped out. I had been on deck twenty hours. Oh, it had been *such* a day! I told Nick to sail another hour while I slept below. Reminded him—he needed no reminding—to look sharp for traffic. Checked the trim, noted our course, noticed the stars fading, overpowered by moonlight. Was halfway below when I thought to say:

"Call me right away if fog comes in."

"Sure, Dad."

I laughed, a little. *Sure, Dad* really meant *Shut up, Dad, trust me.*

In fact, I trust nothing and nobody, including myself. I know a bit about myself, including what I don't know, so I ration trust miserly. I have my compass swung, update charts, tighten what is loose, reef too soon. A thirty percent chance of thunderstorms is one hundred percent to this meteorologist. The only surprise I welcome at sea is a wind shift in my favor. *Uneventful* is my favorite notation in the log. I do not sail boats to pump adrenaline, or to grow an ulcer. When I finally put away the last of many motorcycles, I put to rest whatever compulsion got me speeding tickets. My desideratum at sea is elementary: to cause no harm.

To cause no harm is no passive ambition. It requires an imagination for disaster; it demands that the master of a vessel (or of children, say) not put his vessel (or his family, say) in harm's way, needlessly, fecklessly. I expect to be surprised at sea—I am not a fool (I once thought)—but I want surprise to come of natural law rather than my carelessness.

So you see, the captain of *Blackwing* that moonlit July night in Massachusetts Bay, bound for the Gulf of Maine, was a prudent mariner. Which is why I had felt wounded, unjustly judged, by Priscilla's reservations about this overnight passage, indeed, our first overnight passage as a family. She had sailed with me for twenty years and better than anyone she knew my limits, because we had taught ourselves to sail together, first on day sailers in Chesapeake Bay, then on an Ohlsom 35 yawl we owned with Priscilla's sister and brother-in-law John.

I owe my circumspection at sea to John's negative example. To push the envelope was his only purpose. Many an adventure with John, many a laugh, never a dull afternoon on the water with John, many a bump, many a grounding. I came to hate the damned excitement, and soon I was surprised to discover I had translated myself from the quondam Hotspur Priscilla had married into a very clerk of a sailor, fussy, priggish, a look-before-you-leaper. This fever of caution had alarmingly spread inland to other enterprises: I now balanced my checkbook, "maintained" my shoes, did a fall lay-up on my body, would have put a spring coat of varnish on the lawn mower if I could get the Z-Spar to adhere to grease. Bobbing at a mooring in Buzzards Bay, launchpad for the Cape Cod Canal and points Down East, the last thing I had expected to hear from Priscilla was:

"You know, maybe we shouldn't. Maybe this is too much for us."

I couldn't believe my ears! On the eve of jumping off, having voyaged from Jamestown, Rhode Island, to Wing's Neck, having topped the tanks, iced the chest, stocked the larder, having collected and annotated the charts, having *promised the boys*, and Priscilla wondered, *now*, if this was a "good idea"!

She gave lame reasons: I seemed strung out by the profusion of tasks and charts, and I hadn't seemed to take into account that we were—how should she best put this? —*shorthanded*.

"What in the world do you mean, 'shorthanded'?"

(The marine weatherman was broadcasting from Boston.)

"I'm not competent to do this. Justin is eleven years old, Nick is thirteen . . . "

"Mom, don't call me names . . . "

(. . . humid . . . wind southwest . . .)

"You are thirteen, till day after tomorrow."

(. . . twenty-five percent chance of evening thunderstorms . . .)

"You're forgetting somebody." I said this patiently, not wishing my logic to crush my dear wife.

"Well, let's talk about you. You'll be in effect single-handing more than thirty hours. I trust you, but at night? Offshore?"

"You mean you don't trust me."

"Guys," Justin said.

(*...fog likely by Monday morning in the Gulf of Maine...*)

"We don't *have* to do this," she said. "Your manhood isn't on the line."

Sure. I saw a picture in my mind's eye, beating home over the course I had just traveled, telling them back in Jamestown I'd be needing my mooring this summer after all, the weatherman had said there was an outside chance of fog Down East and, besides, my wife had reminded me that it's difficult to see in the dark. We'd decided we'd prefer to voyage Down East by Subaru. As Priscilla said, my manhood wasn't on the line.

"But we promised the boys," I said.

"Wow," said Nicholas, with considerable justice.

In fact, I'd promised myself (and a hotel keeper) that come noon the day after tomorrow I'd be swinging at a mooring in Tenants Harbor. That is, I didn't care what Priscilla or a Boston weatherman opined about my plan, we were pushing off next morning at first light.

And so we did. Serene dawn passage through the Cape Cod Canal, Race Point right on the money after a fine morning's sail, humpbacks in the afternoon while we ate an estimable lunch delivered cheerfully from the galley to the cockpit. I kept a meticulous log, made a great show of competence. ("No, thanks, I'll skip that beer, I've got a gang of water ahead.") In fact I felt stretched; I fiddled with the RDF, homing in on Race Point. It gave little assurance, its toy compass poorly damped, the null approximate rather than persuasive. I had considered buying Loran C, but at the time to have bought Loran would have been to sacrifice several necessities: the case of Ruinart champagne in the hold, the rooms waiting our arrival at Tenants Harbor, the tape deck Jimmy Buffett required to sing us downhill to Monhegan.

So, there we were, Nick at the helm, Captain Romance below, dead to the world above.

"It's here, Dad."

Nick sounded grim. Oh boy, oh boy, oh boy. Was it ever there! My sleeping bag was heavy with it. My glasses were wet. I wasn't even surprised. Just before I went below, I'd wiped moisture from the compass dome and, when I'd warned Nick to have a care, I could see my breath.

"Did you see other boats?"

"It came so fast, Dad. It didn't roll in, like they say. It wasn't here and then it was here. Like the whales. I was looking at the moon, so *huge,* and then the moon was gone. It just blinked off."

"Did you see anything?" I willed my voice to hold steady. It was 3:35. We were in the Portland shipping lanes. With any luck we would see the loom of the big light on Monhegan in a couple of hours. Maybe we'd get lucky again? Didn't that seem fair?

"There was a set of fast-moving lights to seaward, heading across our bow. Pretty far ahead."

"How far?"

"I don't know, Dad. It's hard to say at night."

So it was.

"Any other shipping?"

"Something on our course, coming up astern. A sailboat, maybe. I don't think it's moving faster than we are."

But we weren't moving. We were becalmed. Nick and I dropped sails and fired up the sturdy Yanmar diesel, never a missed breath these three years. My chest had already cramped, while I waited for some tanker to crawl into our cockpit. I posted Nick in the bow, resumed 040 degrees, smelled coffee brewing. Priscilla was looking through the companionway hatch.

"Priscilla . . ." I began.

"Just keep your head," she said.

How did it get so cold? The rigging dripped on us. The decks were greased with wet and the gray swells seemed oiled. Nick blew a foghorn with requisite regularity into the dense, wet dark, which swallowed the doleful, coarse noise.

Oh, how I had counted on the loom of Monhegan Island light! To follow the loom of that light home to its source was the First Principle of this adventure. Now the light could be fixed to my damned bowsprit and I wouldn't see it.

Hours later, with Justin in the bow blowing a pitiful warning, with Nick below trying to recover from the night, with Priscilla deep in Duncan and Ware's *Cruising Guide to the New England Coast,* day broke. Day broke my heart. Black, impenetrable obscurity had given way to pearly obscurity. Portland marine weather said it was going to be a great day ashore, sunny and hot, good beach day, maybe a little hazy. Oh, offshore? Fog banks. This was told as though it weren't a tragedy, but commonplace!

Priscilla never said, then or later, "How did you get us into this?" But how could I fail to know that she was thinking as she read (Roger F.) Duncan and (John P.) Ware, whose celebration of the water we now blindly bobbed upon bristled with warning labels of treacherous tides, rocky shoals, evil weather, fog?

Priscilla is neither vindictive nor eager to make a bad situation worse, but she read aloud from the humid pages something she thought I might need to know: "'The onshore tide set from Portsmouth onward is a major navigation hazard. In spite of the fact that we make a major compensation for this effect, we almost always fall inside of the anticipated landfall. . . . '"

"Does that bear on us?" Priscilla asked.

I nodded. I shook my head. I said, "I don't know." Because the tide sets irregularly along the course we had sailed, in a circular motion, I hadn't the least notion where I was, not the foggiest. Now I favored east over north, the sea over the coast. The good news: I wouldn't (probably) run up on a rocky beach in Muscongus Bay. The bad news: Between us and Portugal were few bells, horns, whistles.

At 10:00 A.M., our ETA for Monhegan, the diesel coughed and then it sputtered. Nick was at the helm and I barked at him, thinking (I guess) he'd adjusted the throttle, which he hadn't. For the first time with my family at sea, I had shouted in panic and my response provoked alarm in the people I had brought here to make happy. I felt sorry for myself; I was ashamed; I was scared.

I'd been in fog before, fog as thick as this. I'd never been in fog thicker than this, because fog didn't get thicker than this, but I'd run buoy to buoy from Pulpit Harbor on North Haven into Camden. That was five years ago, and when I'd missed a mark, I'd known enough to motor the boundaries of a square, shutting off the engine to listen, and I'd found my way. It had been a strain, of course, cramping the neck muscles, all that tensing to hear, that fierce concentration on the compass. We'd been swallowed by fog running from Block Island to Newport, Rhode Island, and I hadn't panicked, just patiently held on course for Brenton Tower and there it was, its monster spider legs rising from the sea, on the button.

This was different. I tried to find Monhegan with the laughable RDF. The null suggested it was abeam, either port or starboard. Gee, thanks. The weather radio suggested a likely possibility of thunderstorms and we prayed for them, to blow the fog away, to part the veil for just a moment. The air was milky, like sour milk, dreadful yellow. The air was thick, morose. We were cold. A slight breeze astern blew diesel exhaust at us.

We didn't speak. I think they were ashamed for me. We listened. Will I ever listen as acutely? I dared not shut off the engine. Why? I can't remember. I believed so powerfully now in entropy—in general disintegration and systematic failure, in bad luck—that I dared not alter anything: course, throttle, helmsman. We motored forward, 040 degrees. . . .

o   o   o

Priscilla heard it first. Then I heard it and throttled back after all, and then we all heard it, a low moan, like someone sick. The delicate lament would come and go. For an hour we sought it, steering every which way, finally finding our way to it. My rational self knew that a whistle had not been placed to tell us where we were but to mark a hazard; I knew no hazard worse than not knowing where we were. Nick begged me to come up on it slow and I did, because I was stalking the whistle and feared I'd spook it. And there it was, fifty feet, anchored. I envied it. Now the deep whistle groaned frankly, excessively.

We circled it while I called the Coast Guard; my voice alarmed me. I had once had a bad stutter and it had come back. Was there an "SL," black and white, near Monhegan?

That was a negative, Skipper. We were circling a marker on the Seal Ledges, a little east of Large Green Island, fourteen nautical miles east-northeast of Monhegan, which we had missed by a mile (as they say). We were in bad water, with a foot between our keel and a kelpy rock slab, and the Coast Guard suggested we get ourselves out of there, pronto, to Matinicus Island, three miles east.

Looking back, I guess we should have felt rescued. But our least desired course that afternoon was a course to seaward that would leave behind us the one thing we knew, yonder moaning whistle.

The weather radio was undecided between thunderstorms and dense fog, growing denser. We went for Matinicus and its sister a little to seaward—Ragged—trying to pick up a nun on the Foster Ledges, missing it (big surprise). We should have been near Matinicus. Priscilla was reading:

"'. . . the region should be approached with caution. There are no really snug harbors . . . unmarked dangers are frequent and tides are swift. In fog or storm the careless or inexperienced can get into real trouble. . . .'"

Justin was on the bowsprit, shouting, "Look at those thunderclouds!"

I looked up and saw black. Umbrella pines on a cliff. And then we were among the rocks and a rocky beach materialized yards ahead, and I swung the wheel over while Nick yelled directions, and we *didn't* tear open the hull, or ground, or even stub our toe.

We anchored. I got on the radio (and this hurts to repeat):

"Anybody on Ragged Island or Matinicus. Please come back. This is *Blackwing*. I am off a rocky beach on the west side of one of your islands. We are tired and lost. I repeat, we are frightened. Please come back."

And bingo, back came a lobsterman. Said he was pulling pots, he had us on his radar, would drop by in a jiffy, lead us into Criehaven, the harbor on Ragged. He had an extra mooring, he said, we could use it. Drink a cup of coffee, he suggested. Take it easy. Welcome to Maine, he said.

I don't think Priscilla will mind if I tell she fell in love with that lobsterman before she met him. Did I resent how Priscilla and my sons felt about the man with radar and sense enough to find his way (and ours) to a safe haven? I did not. My manhood, poor pathetic thing, was back there in the Portland shipping lanes, or where I'd lost my wits somewhere near Monhegan, when I forgot how to use an RDF, where I'd gone plumb dumb, numb with senseless dread.

When the lobsterman came alongside and saw how it was, heard my voice and saw my hands shaking, he suggested, seeing how thick o' fog it was, that he would *tow* us

in. That seemed to me a capital notion, jus[t]
idea anyone ever had. He towed, I pretended [to]
boys fished off the stern and hauled them in, laug[h]

We hung on a mooring in Criehaven two day[s]
nights. It's a snug harbor, but till the fog lifted we nev[er]
saw land from *Blackwing*. That night it cleared and we
saw the Northern Lights. Next morning: fog. We stayed
put. If the fog hadn't lifted we'd still be there, believe me.
But the fog did lift, as it does, and we moved along, and
Maine showed us a dandy time.

So now? I feel less and less like a fool, which is
striking evidence of foolishness. More and more it seems
fine and sensible to try it again. Next time I'd like to creep
up on Matinicus Rock at dawn and surprise the puffins.
With Loran, of course. Matinicus Rock is almost as easy a
chance from Race Point as Monhegan. After all, *Blackwing*
came through. We did. Where was the harm?

the brightest
o steer, the
hing.
two
er

AROUND THE CAPE
PAUL THEROUX

The boat slid down the bank and without a splash into the creek, which was gray this summer morning. The air was woolly with mist. The tide had turned, but just a moment ago, so there was still no motion on the water—no current, not a ripple. The marsh grass was a deeper green for there being no sun. It was as if—this early and this dark—the day had not yet begun to breathe.

I straightened the boat and took my first stroke: the gurgle of the spoon blades and the sigh of the twisting oarlock were the only sounds. I set off, moving like a water bug through the marsh and down the bendy creek to the sea. When my strokes were regular and I was rowing at a good clip, my mind started to work, and I thought: *I'm not coming back tonight.* And so the day seemed long enough and full of possibilities. I had no plans except to keep on harbor-hopping around the Cape, and it was easy now going out with the tide.

This was Scorton Creek, in East Sandwich, and our hill—one of the few on the low, lumpy terminal moraine of the Cape—was once an Indian fort. Wampanoags. The local farmers plowed this hill until recently, when the houses went up, and their plow blades always struck flints and ax heads and beads. I splashed past a boathouse the size of a garage. When they dug the foundation for that boathouse less than twenty years ago, they unearthed a large male Wampanoag who had been buried in a sitting position, his skin turned to leather and his bones sticking through. They slung him out and put the boathouse there.

Three more bends in the creek and I could see the current stirring more strongly around me. A quarter of a mile away in the marsh was a Great Blue Heron—five feet high and moving in a slow prayerful way, like a narrow-shouldered priest in gray vestments. The boat slipped along, carrying itself between strokes. Up ahead on the beach was a person with a dog—one of those energetic early risers who boasts, "I only need four hours' sleep!" and is probably hell to live with. Nothing else around—only the terns screeching over their eggs, and a few boats motionless at their moorings, and a rather crummy clutter of beach houses and NO TRESPASSING signs, and the ghosts of dead Indians. The current was so swift in the creek I couldn't have gone back if I tried, and as I approached the shore it shot me into the sea. And now light was dazzling in the mist, as on the magnificent Turner *Sunrise with Seamonsters*.

After an hour I was at Sandy Neck Public Beach—about four miles. This bay side of the upper Cape has a low duney shore and notoriously shallow water in places. The half a dozen harbors are spread over seventy miles and most have dangerous bars. It is not a coast for easy cruising and in many areas there is hardly enough water for windsurfing. There are sand bars in the oddest places. Most sailboats can't approach any of the harbors unless the tide is high. So the little boats stay near shore and watch the tides, and the deep draft boats stay miles offshore. I was in between and I was alone. In two months of this I never saw another rowboat more than fifty yards from the shore. Indeed, I seldom saw anyone rowing at all.

Sandy Neck proper, an eight-mile peninsula of Arabian-style dunes, was today a panorama of empty beach; the only life stirring was the gulls and more distantly the hovering marsh hawks. A breeze had come up; it had freshened; it was now a light wind. I got stuck on a sand bar, then hopped out and dragged the boat into deeper water. I was trying to get around Beach Point to have my lunch in Barnstable Harbor—my forward locker contained provisions. I was frustrated by the shoals. But I should have known—there were seagulls all over the ocean here and they were not swimming but standing. I grew to recognize low water from the posture of seagulls.

When I drew level with Barnstable Harbor I was spun around by the strong current. I had to fight it for half an hour before I got ashore. Even then I was only at Beach Point. This was the channel into the harbor, and the water in it was narrow and swiftly moving—a deep river flowing through a shallow sea, its banks just submerged.

I tied the boat to a rock, and while I rested a Ranger drove up in his Chevy Bronco.

He said, "That wind's picking up. I think we're in for a storm." He pointed toward Barnstable Harbor. "See the clouds building up over there? The forecast said showers but that looks like more than showers. Might be a thunderstorm. Where are you headed?"

"Just up the coast."

He nodded at the swiftly rushing channel and said, "You'll have to get across that thing first."

"Why is it so choppy?"

His explanation was simple, and it accounted for a great deal of the rough water I was to see in the weeks to come. He said that when the wind was blowing in the opposite direction to a tide, a chop of hard, irregular waves was whipped up. It could become very fierce very quickly.

Then he pointed across the harbor mouth toward Bass Hole and told me to look at how the ebbing tide had uncovered a mile of sand flats. "At low tide people just walk around over there," he said. So, beyond the vicious channel the sea was slipping down—white water here, none there.

After the Ranger drove off, I made myself a cheese sandwich, swigged some coffee from my thermos bottle, and decided to rush the channel. My skiff's sides were lapstrake—like clapboards—and rounded, which stabilized the boat in high waves, but this short breaking chop was a different matter. Instead of rowing at right angles to the current I turned the bow against it, and steadied the skiff by rowing. The skiff rocked wildly—the current slicing the bow, the wind-driven chop smacking the stern. A few minutes later I was across. And then I ran aground. After the channel were miles of watery shore; but it was only a few inches deep—and the tide was still dropping.

The wind was blowing, the sky was dark, the shoreline was distant; and now the water was not deep enough for this rowboat. I got out and—watched by strolling seagulls—dragged the boat through the shallow water that lay over the sand bar. The boat skidded and sometimes floated, but it was not really buoyant until I had splashed along for about an hour. To anyone on the beach I must have seemed a bizarre figure—alone, far from shore, walking on the water.

It was midafternoon by the time I had dragged the boat to deeper water, and I got in and began to row. The wind seemed to be blowing now from the west; it gathered at the stern and gave me a following sea, lifting me in the direction I wanted to go. I rowed past Chapin Beach and the bluffs, and around the black rocks at Nobscusset Harbor, marking my progress on my flapping chart by glancing again and again at a water tower like a stovepipe in Dennis.

At about five o'clock I turned into Sesuit Harbor, still pulling hard. I had rowed about sixteen miles. My hands were blistered but I had made a good start. And I had made a discovery: the sea was unpredictable, and the shore looked foreign. I was used to finding familiar things in exotic places, but the unfamiliar at home was new to me. It had been a disorienting day. At times I had been afraid. It was a taste of something strange in a place I had known my whole life. It was a shock and a satisfaction.

Mrs. Coffin at Sesuit Harbor advised me not to go out the next day. Anyone with a name out of *Moby-Dick* is worth listening to on the subject of the sea. The wind was blowing from the northeast, making Mrs. Coffin's flag snap and beating the sea into whitecaps.

I said, "I'm only going to Rock Harbor."

It was about nine miles.

She said, "You'll be pulling your guts out."

I decided to go, thinking: *I would rather struggle in a heavy sea and get wet than sit in the harbor and wait for the weather to improve.*

But as soon as I had rowed beyond the breakwater I was hit hard by the waves and tipped by the wind. I unscrewed my sliding seat and jammed the thwart into place; and I tried again. I couldn't maneuver the boat. I changed oars, lashing the long ones down and using the seven-and-a-half-foot ones. I made some progress, but the wind was punching me toward shore. This was West Brewster, off Quivett Neck. The chart showed church spires. I rowed for another few hours and saw that I had gone hardly any distance at all. But there was no point in turning back. I didn't need a harbor. I knew I could beach the boat anywhere—pull it up over there at that ramp, or between those rocks, or at that public beach. I had plenty of time and I felt all right. This was like walking uphill, but so what?

So I struggled all day. I hated the banging waves, and the way they leaped over the sides when the wind pushed me sideways into the troughs of the swell. There was a few inches of water sloshing in the bottom, and my chart was soaked. At noon a motorboat came near me and asked me if I was in trouble. I said no and told him where I was going. The man said, "Rock Harbor's real far!" and pointed east. Some of the seawater dried on the boat, leaving the lace of crystallized salt shimmering on the mahogany. I pulled on, passing a sailboat in the middle of the afternoon.

"Where's Rock Harbor?" I asked.

"Look for the trees!"

But I looked in the wrong place. The trees weren't on shore, they were in the water, about twelve of them planted in two rows—tall dead limbless pines—like lampposts. They marked the harbor entrance; they also marked the Brewster Flats, for at low tide there was no water here at all, and Rock Harbor was just a creek draining into a desert of sand. You could drive a car across the harbor mouth at low tide.

I had arranged to meet my father here. My brother Joseph was with him. He had just arrived from the Pacific islands of Samoa. I showed him the boat.

He touched the oarlocks. He said, "They're all tarnished." Then he frowned at the salt-smeared wood and his gaze made the boat seem small and rather puny.

I said, "I just rowed from Sesuit with the wind against me. It took me the whole goddamned day!"

He said, "Don't get excited."

"What do you know about boats?" I said.

He went silent. We got into the car—two boys and their father. I had not seen Joe for several years. Perhaps he was sulking because I hadn't asked about Samoa. But had he asked about my rowing? It didn't seem like much, because it was travel at home. Yet I felt the day had been full of risks.

"How the hell," I said, "can you live in Samoa for eight years and not know anything about boats?"

"*Sah*-moa," he said, correcting my pronunciation. It was a family joke.

My brother Alex was waiting with my mother, and he smiled as I entered the house.

"Here he comes," Alex said.

My face was burned, the blisters had broken on my hands and left them raw, my back ached, and so did the muscle strings in my forearm; there was sea salt in my eyes.

"Ishmael," Alex said. He was sitting compactly on a chair glancing narrowly at me and smoking. "'And I only am escaped alone to tell thee.'"

My mother said, "We're almost ready to eat—you must be starving! God, look at you!"

Alex was behind her. He made a face at me, then silently mimicked a laugh at the absurdity of a forty-two-year-old man taking consolation from his mother.

"Home is the sailor, home from the sea," Alex said and imitated my voice, "Pass the spaghetti, Mom!"

Joe had started to relax. Now he had an ally, and I was being mocked. We were not writers, husbands, or fathers. We were three big boys fooling in front of their parents. Home is so often the simple past.

"What's he been telling you, Joe?" Alex asked.

I went to wash my face.

"He said I don't know anything about boats."

Just before we sat down to eat, I said, "It's pretty rough out there."

Alex seized on this, looking delighted. He made the sound of a strong wind, by whistling and clearing his throat. He squinted and in a harsh whisper said, "Aye, it's rough out there, and you can hardly"—he stood up, banging the dining table with his thigh—"you can hardly see the bowsprit. Aye, and the wind's shifting, too. But never mind, Mr. Christian! Give him twenty lashes—that'll take the strut out of him! And hoist the mainsail—we're miles from anywhere. None of you swabbies knows anything about boats. But I know, because I've sailed from Pitcairn Island to Rock Harbor by dead reckoning—in the roughest water known to man. Just me against the elements, with the waves threatening to pitch-pole my frail craft..."

"Your supper's getting cold," Father said.

"How long did it take you?" Mother said to me.

"All day," I said.

"Aye, captain," Alex said. "Aw, it's pretty rough out there, what with the wind and the rising sea."

"What will you write about?" my father asked.

"He'll write about ocean's roar and how he just went around the Horn. You're looking at Francis Chichester! The foam beating against the wheelhouse, the mainsheet screaming, the wind and the rising waves. Hark! Thunder and lightning over *The Gypsy Moth*!"

Declaiming made Alex imaginative, and stirred his memory. He had an actor's gift for sudden shouts and whispers and for giving himself wholly to the speech. It was as if he was on an instant touched with lucid insanity, the exalted chaos of creation. He was triumphant.

"But look at him now—Peter Freuchen of the seven seas, the old tar in his clinker-built boat. He's home asking his mother to pass the spaghetti! 'Thanks, Mom, I'd love another helping, Mom.' After a day in the deep sea, he's with his mother and father, reaching for the meatballs!"

Joseph was laughing hard, his whole body swelling as he tried to suppress it.

"He's not going to write about that. No, nothing about the spaghetti. It'll just be Captain Bligh, all alone, bending at his oars, and picking oakum through the long tumultuous nights at sea. And the wind and the murderous waves..."

"Dry up," Father said, still eating.

Then they all turned their big sympathetic faces at me across the cluttered dining table. Alex looked slightly sheepish, and the others apprehensive, fearing that I might be offended, that Alex had gone too far.

"What will you write about?" Mother asked.

I shook my head and tried not to smile—because I was thinking: *That.*

S.O.S.°

SHIP-
WR

ECKS

SURVIVOR TYPE
STEPHEN KING

Sooner or later the question comes up in every medical student's career. How much shock-trauma can the patient stand? Different instructors answer the question in different ways, but cut to its base level, the answer is always another question: *How badly does the patient want to survive?*

January 26

Two days since the storm washed me up. I paced the island off just this morning. Some island! It is 190 paces wide at its thickest point, and 267 paces long from tip to tip.

So far as I can tell, there is nothing on it to eat.

My name is Richard Pine. This is my diary. If I'm found (when), I can destroy this easily enough. There is no shortage of matches. Matches and heroin. Plenty of both. Neither of them worth doodly-squat here, ha-ha. So I will write. It will pass the time, anyway.

If I'm to tell the whole truth—and why not? I sure have the time!—I'll have to start by saying I was born Richard Pinzetti, in New York's Little Italy. My father was an Old World guinea. I wanted to be a surgeon. My father would laugh, call me crazy, and tell me to get him another glass of wine. He died of cancer when he was forty-six. I was glad.

I played football in high school. I was the best damn football player my school ever produced. Quarterback. I made All-City my last two years. I hated football. But if you're a poor wop from the projects and you want to go to college, sports are your only ticket. So I played, and I got my athletic scholarship.

In college I only played ball until my grades were good enough to get a full academic scholarship. Pre-med. My father died six weeks before graduation. Good deal. Do you think I wanted to walk across that stage and get my diploma and look down and see that fat greaseball sitting there? Does a hen want a flag? I got into a fraternity, too. It wasn't one of the good ones, not with a name like Pinzetti, but a fraternity all the same.

Why am I writing this? It's almost funny. No, I take that back. It *is* funny. The great Dr. Pine, sitting on a rock in his pajama bottoms and a T-shirt, sitting on an island almost small enough to spit across, writing his life story. Am I hungry! Never mind, I'll write my goddam life story if I want to. At least it keeps my mind off my stomach. Sort of.

I changed my name to Pine before I started med school. My mother said I was breaking her heart. What heart? The day after my old man was in the ground, she was out hustling that Jew grocer down at the end of the block.

For someone who loved the name so much, she was in one hell of a hurry to change her copy of it to Steinbrunner.

Surgery was all I ever wanted. Ever since high school. Even then I was wrapping my hands before every game and soaking them afterward. If you want to be a surgeon, you have to take care of your hands. Some of the kids used to rag me about it, call me chickenshit. I never fought them. Playing football was risk enough. But there were ways. The one that got on my case the most was Howie Plotsky, a big dumb bohunk with zits all over his face. I had a paper route, and I was selling the numbers along with the papers. I had a little coming in lots of ways. You get to know people, you listen, you make connections. You have to, when you're hustling the streets. Any asshole knows how to die. The thing to learn is how to survive, you know what I mean? So I paid the biggest kid in school, Ricky Brazzi, ten bucks to make Howie Plotsky's mouth disappear. Make it disappear, I said. I will pay you a dollar for every tooth you bring me. Rico brought me three teeth wrapped up in a paper towel. He dislocated two of his knuckles doing the job, so you see the kind of trouble I could have got into.

In med school while the other suckers were running themselves ragged trying to bone up—no pun intended, ha-ha—between waiting tables or selling neckties or buffing floors, I kept the rackets going. Football pools, basketball pools, a little policy. I stayed on good terms with the old neighborhood. And I got through school just fine.

I didn't get into pushing until I was doing my residency. I was working in one of the biggest hospitals in New

York City. At first it was just prescriptions blanks. I'd sell a tablet of a hundred blanks to some guy from the neighborhood, and he'd forge the names of forty or fifty different doctors on them, using writing samples I'd also sell him. The guy would turn around and peddle the blanks on the street for ten or twenty dollars apiece. The speed freaks and the nodders loved it.

And after a while I found out just how much of a balls-up the hospital drug room was in. Nobody knew what was coming in or going out. There were people lugging the goodies out by the double handfuls. Not me. I was always careful. I never got into trouble until I got careless—and unlucky. But I'm going to land on my feet. I always do.

Can't write any more now. My wrist's tired and the pencil's dull. I don't know why I'm bothering, anyway. Somebody'll probably pick me up soon.

January 27

The boat drifted away last night and sank in about ten feet of water off the north side of the island. Who gives a rip? The bottom was like Swiss cheese after coming over the reef anyway. I'd already taken off anything that was worth taking. Four gallons of water. A sewing kit. A first-aid kit. This book I'm writing in, which is supposed to be a lifeboat inspection log. That's a laugh. Whoever heard of a lifeboat with no FOOD on it? The last report written in here is August 9, 1970. Oh, yes, two knives, one dull and one fairly sharp, one combination fork and spoon. I'll use them when I eat my supper tonight. Roast rock. Ha-ha. Well, I did get my pencil sharpened.

When I get off this pile of guano-splattered rock, I'm going to sue the bloody hell out of Paradise Lines, Inc. That alone is worth living for. And I am going to live. I'm going to get out of this. Make no mistake about it. I am going to get out of this.

(later)

When I was making my inventory, I forgot one thing: two kilos of pure heroin, worth about $350,000, New York street value. Here it's worth el zilcho. Sort of funny, isn't it? Ha-ha!

January 28

Well, I've eaten—if you want to call that eating. There was a gull perched on one of the rocks at the center of the island. The rocks are all jumbled up into a kind of mini-mountain there—all covered with birdshit, too. I got a chunk of stone that just fitted into my hand and climbed up as close to it as I dared. It just stood there on its rock, watching me with its bright black eyes. I'm surprised that the rumbling of my stomach didn't scare it off.

I threw the rock as hard as I could and hit it broadside. It let out a loud squawk and tried to fly away, but I'd broken its right wing. I scrambled up after it and it hopped away. I could see the blood trickling over its white feathers. The son of a bitch led me a merry chase; once, on the other side of the central rockpile, I got my foot caught in a hole between two rocks and nearly fractured my ankle.

It began to tire at last, and I finally caught it on the east side of the island. It was actually trying to get into the water and paddle away. I caught a handful of its tailfeathers and it turned around and pecked me. Then I had one hand around its feet. I got my other hand on its miserable neck and broke it. The sound gave me great satisfaction. Lunch is served, you know? Ha! Ha!

I carried it back to my "camp," but even before I plucked and gutted it, I used iodine to swab the laceration its beak had made. Birds carry all sorts of germs, and the last thing I need now is an infection.

The operation on the gull went quite smoothly. I could not cook it, alas. Absolutely no vegetation or driftwood on the island and the boat has sunk. So I ate it raw. My stomach wanted to regurgitate it immediately. I sympathized but could not allow it. I counted backward until the nausea passed. It almost always works.

Can you imagine that bird, almost breaking my ankle and then pecking me? If I catch another one tomorrow, I'll torture it. I let this one off too easily. Even as I write, I am able to glance down at its severed head on the sand. Its black eyes, even with the death-glaze on them, seem to be mocking me.

Do gulls have brains in any quantity?

Are they edible?

January 29

No chow today. One gull landed near the top of the rockpile but flew off before I could get close enough to "throw it a forward pass," ha-ha! I've started a beard. Itches like hell. If the gull comes back and I get it, I'm going to cut its eyes out before I kill it.

I was one hell of a surgeon, as I believe I may have said. They drummed me out. It's a laugh, really; they all do it, and they're so bloody sanctimonious when someone gets caught at it. Screw you, Jack, I got mine. The Second Oath of Hippocrates and Hypocrites.

I had enough socked away from my adventures as an intern and a resident (that's supposed to be like an officer and a gentlemen according to the Oath of Hypocrites, but don't you believe it) to set myself up in practice on Park Avenue. A good thing for me, too; I had no rich daddy or established patron, as so many of my "colleagues" did. By the time my shingle was out, my father was nine years in his pauper's grave. My mother died the year before my license to practice was revoked.

It was a kickback thing. I had a deal going with half a dozen East Side pharmacists, with two drug supply houses, and with at least twenty other doctors. Patients were sent to me and I sent patients. I performed operations and prescribed the correct procedures, and all the operations were necessary, but I never performed one against a patient's will. And I never had a patient look down at what was written on the prescription blank and say, "I don't want this." Listen: they'd have a hysterectomy in 1965 or a partial thyroid in 1970, and still be taking painkillers five or ten years later, if you'd let them. Sometimes I did. I wasn't the only one, you know. They could afford the habit. And sometimes a patient would have trouble sleeping after minor surgery. Or trouble getting diet pills. Or Librium. It could all be arranged. Ha! Yes! If they hadn't gotten it from me, they would have gotten it from someone else.

Then the tax people got to Lowenthal. That sheep. They waved five years in his face and he coughed up a half a dozen names. One of them was mine. They watched me for a while, and by the time they landed, I was worth a lot more than five years. There were a few other deals, including the prescription blanks, which I hadn't given up entirely. It's funny, I didn't really need that stuff anymore, but it was a habit. Hard to give up that extra sugar.

Well, I knew some people. I pulled some strings. And I threw a couple of people to the wolves. Nobody I liked, though. Everyone I gave to the feds was a real son of a bitch.

Christ, I'm hungry.

January 30

No gulls today. Reminds me of the signs you'd sometimes see on the pushcarts back in the neighborhood. NO TOMA-TOES TODAY. I walked out into the water up to my waist with the sharp knife in my hand. I stood completely still in that one place with the sun beating down on me for four hours. Twice I thought I was going to faint, but I counted backward until it passed. I didn't see one fish. Not one.

January 31

Killed another gull, the same way I did the first. I was too hungry to torture it the way I had been promising myself. I gutted and ate it. Squeezed the tripes and then ate them, too. It's strange how you can feel your vitality surge back. I was beginning to get scared there, for a while. Lying in the shade of the big central rockpile, I'd think I was hearing voices. My father. My mother. My ex-wife. And worst of all the big Chink who sold me the heroin in Saigon. He had a lisp, possibly from a partially cleft palate.

"Go ahead," his voice came out of nowhere. "Go ahead and thnort a little. You won't notith how hungry you are then. It'h beautiful . . . " But I've never done dope, not even sleeping pills.

Lowenthal killed himself, did I tell you that? That sheep. He hanged himself in what used to be his office. The way I look at it, he did the world a favor.

I wanted my shingle back. Some of the people I talked to said it could be done—but it would cost big money. More grease than I'd ever dreamed of. I had $40,000 in a safe-deposit box. I decided I'd have to take a chance and try to turn it over. Double or triple it.

So I went to see Ronnie Hanelli. Ronnie and I played football together in college, and when his kid brother decided on internal med, I helped him get a residency. Ronnie himself was in pre-law, how's that for funny? On the block when we were growing up we called him Ronnie the Enforcer because he umped all the stickball games and reffed the hockey. If you didn't like his calls, you had your choice—you could keep your mouth shut or you could eat knuckles. The Puerto Ricans called him *Ronniewop*. All one word like that. *Ronniewop*. Used to tickle him. And that guy went to college, and then to law school, and he breezed through his bar exam the first time he took it, and then he set up shop in the old neighborhood, right over the Fish Bowl Bar. I close my eyes and I can still see him cruising down the block in that white Continental of his. The biggest fucking loan shark in the city.

I knew Ronnie would have something for me. "It's dangerous," he said. "But you could always take care of yourself. And if you can get the stuff back in, I'll introduce you to a couple of fellows. One of them is a state representative."

He gave me two names over there. One of them was the big Chink, Henry Li-Tsu. The other was a Vietnamese named Solom Ngo. A chemist. For a fee he would test the Chink's product. The Chink was known to play "jokes" from time to time. The "jokes" were plastic bags filled with talcum powder, with drain cleaner, with cornstarch. Ronnie said that one day Li-Tsu's little jokes would get him killed.

February 1

There was a plane. It flew right across the island. I tried to climb to the top of the rockpile and wave to it. My foot went into a hole. The same damn hole I got it stuck in the day I killed the first bird, I think. I've fractured my ankle, compound fracture. It went like a gunshot. The pain was unbelievable. I screamed and lost my balance, pinwheeling my arms like a madman, but I went down and hit my head and everything went black. I didn't wake up until dusk. I lost some blood where I hit my head. My ankle had swelled up like a tire, and I'd got myself a very nasty sunburn. I think if there had been another hour of sun, it would have blistered.

Dragged myself back here and spent last night shivering and crying with frustration. I disinfected the head wound, which is just above the right temporal lobe, and bandaged it as well as I could. Just a superficial scalp wound plus minor concussion, I think, but the ankle . . . it's a bad break, involved in two places, possibly three.

How will I chase the birds now?

It had to be a plane looking for survivors from the *Callas*. In the dark and the storm, the lifeboat must have carried miles from where it sank. They may not be back this way.

God, my ankle hurts so bad.

February 2

I made a sign on the small white shingle of a beach on the island's south side, where the lifeboat grounded. It took me all day, with pauses to rest in the shade. Even so, I fainted twice. As a guess, I'd say I've lost 25 lbs, mostly from dehydration. But now, from where I sit, I can see the four letters it took me all day to spell out; dark rocks against the white sand, they say HELP in characters four feet high. Another plane won't miss me.

If there is another plane.

My foot throbs constantly. There is swelling still and ominous discoloration around the double break. Discoloration seems to have advanced. Binding it tightly with my shirt alleviates the worst of the pain, but it's still bad enough so that I faint rather than sleep.

I have begun to think I may have to amputate.

February 3

Swelling and discoloration worse still. I'll wait until tomorrow. If the operation does become necessary, I believe I can carry it through. I have matches for sterilizing the sharp knife, I have needle and thread from the sewing kit. My shirt for a bandage.

I even have two kilo of "painkiller," although hardly of the type I used to prescribe. But they would have taken it if they could have gotten it. You bet. Those old blue-haired ladies would have snorted Glade air freshener if they thought it would have gotten them high. Believe it!

February 4

I've decided to amputate my foot. No food four days now. If I wait any longer, I run the risk of fainting from combined shock and hunger in the middle of the operation and bleeding to death. And as wretched as I am, I still want to live. I remember what Mockridge used to say in Basic Anatomy. Old Mockie, we used to call him. Sooner or later, he'd say, the question comes up in every medical student's career: How much shock-trauma can the patient stand? And he'd whack his pointer at his chart of the human body, hitting the liver, the kidneys, the heart, the spleen, the intestines. Cut to its base level, gentlemen, he'd say, the answer is always another question: How badly does the patient want to survive?

I think I can bring it off.

I really do.

I suppose I'm writing to put off the inevitable, but it did occur to me that I haven't finished the story of how I came to be here. Perhaps I should tie up that loose end in case the operation does go badly. It will only take a few minutes, and I'm sure there will be enough daylight left for the operation, for, according to my Pulsar, it's only nine past nine in the morning. Ha!

I flew to Saigon as a tourist. Does that sound strange? It shouldn't. There are still thousands of people who visit there every year in spite of Nixon's war. There are people who go to see car wrecks and cockfights, too.

My Chinese friend had the merchandise. I took it to Ngo, who pronounced it very high-grade stuff. He told me that Li-Tsu had played one of his jokes four months ago and that his wife had been blown up when she turned on the ignition of her Opel. Since then there had been no more jokes.

I stayed in Saigon for three weeks; I had booked passage back to San Francisco on a cruise ship, the *Callas*. First cabin. Getting on board with the merchandise was no trouble; for a fee Ngo arranged for two customs officials to simply wave me on after running through my suitcases. The merchandise was in an airline flight bag, which they never even looked at.

"Getting through U.S. Customs will be much more difficult," Ngo told me. "That, however, is your problem."

I had no intention of taking the merchandise through U.S. Customs. Ronnie Hanelli had arranged for a skin diver who would do a certain rather tricky job for $3,000. I was to meet him (two days ago, now that I think of it) in a San Francisco flophouse called the St. Regis Hotel. The plan was to put the merchandise in a waterproof can. Attached to the top was a timer and a packet of red dye. Just before we docked, the canister was to be thrown overboard—but not by me, of course.

I was still looking for a cook or a steward who could use a little extra cash and who was smart enough—or stupid enough—to keep his mouth closed afterward, when the *Callas* sank.

I don't know how or why. It was storming, but the ship seemed to be handling that well enough. Around eight o'clock on the evening of the 23rd, there was an explosion somewhere belowdecks. I was in the lounge at the time, and the *Callas* began to list almost immediately. To the left . . . do they call that "port" or "starboard"?

People were screaming and running in every direction. Bottles were falling off the backbar and shattering on the floor. A man staggered up from one of the lower levels, his shirt burned off, his skin barbecued. The loudspeaker started telling people to go the lifeboat stations they had been assigned during the drill at the beginning of the cruise. The passengers went right on running hither and yon. Very few of them had bothered to show up during the lifeboat drill. I not only showed up, I came early—I wanted to be in the front row, you see, so I would have an unobstructed view of everything. I always pay close attention when the matter concerns my own skin.

I went down to my stateroom, got the heroin bags, and put one in each of my front pockets. Then I went to Lifeboat Station 8. As I went up the stairwell to the main deck there were two more explosions and the boat began to list even more severely.

Topside, everything was confusion. I saw a screeching woman with a baby in her arms run past me, gaining speed as she sprinted down the slippery, canting deck. She hit the rail with her thighs, and flipped outward. I saw her do two midair somersaults and part of a third before I lost sight of her. There was a middle-aged man sitting in the center of the shuffleboard court and pulling hair. Another man in cook's whites, horribly burned about his face and hands, was stumbling from place to place and screaming, "HELP ME! CAN'T SEE! HELP ME! CAN'T SEE!"

The panic was almost total: it had run from the passengers to the crew like a disease. You must remember that the time elapsed from the first explosion to the actual sinking of the *Callas* was only about twenty minutes. Some of the lifeboat stations were clogged with screaming passengers, while others were absolutely empty. Mine, on the listing side of the ship, was almost deserted. There was no one there but myself and a common sailor with a pimply, pallid face.

"Let's get this buckety-bottomed old whore in the water," he said, his eyes rolling crazily in their sockets. "This bloody tub is going straight to the bottom."

The lifeboat gear is simple enough to operate, but in his fumbling nervousness, he got his side of the block and tackle tangled. The boat dropped six feet and then hung up, the bow two feet lower than the stern.

I was coming around to help him when he began to scream. He'd succeeded in untangling the snarl and had gotten his hand caught at the same time. The whizzing rope smoked over his open palm, flaying off skin, and he was jerked over the side.

I tossed the rope ladder overboard, hurried down it, and unclipped the lifeboat from the lowering ropes. Then I rowed, something I had occasionally done for pleasure on trips to my friends' summer houses, something I was now doing for my life. I knew that if I didn't get far enough away from the dying *Callas* before she sank, she would pull me down with her.

Just five minutes later she went. I hadn't escaped the suction entirely; I had to row madly just to stay in the same place. She went under very quickly. There were still people clinging to the rail of her bow and screaming. They looked like a bunch of monkeys.

The storm worsened. I lost one oar but managed to keep the other. I spent that whole night in a kind of dream, first bailing, then grabbing the oar and paddling wildly to get the boat's prow into the next bulking wave.

Sometime before dawn on the 24th, the waves began to strengthen behind me. The boat rushed forward. It was terrifying but at the same time exhilarating. Suddenly most of the planking was ripped out from under my feet, but before the lifeboat could sink it was dumped on this godforsaken pile of rocks. I don't even know where I am; have no idea at all. Navigation not my strong point, ha-ha.

But I know what I have to do. This may be the last entry, but somehow I think I'll make it. Haven't I always? And they are really doing marvelous things with prosthetics these days. I can get along with one foot quite nicely.

It's time to see if I'm as good as I think I am. Luck.

February 5
Did it.

The pain was the part I was most worried about. I can stand pain, but I thought that in my weakened condition, a combination of hunger and agony might force unconsciousness before I could finish.

But the heroin solved that quite nicely.

I opened one of the bags and sniffed two healthy pinches from the surface of a flat rock—first the right nostril, then the left. It was like sniffing up some beautifully numbing ice that spread through the brain from the bottom up. I aspirated the heroin as soon as I finished writing in this diary yesterday—that was at 9:45. The next time I checked my watch the shadows had moved, leaving me partially in the sun, and the time was 12:41. I had nodded off. I had never dreamed that it could be so beautiful, and I can't understand why I was so scornful before. The pain, the terror, the misery. . . they all disappear, leaving only a calm euphoria.

It was in this state that I operated.

There was, indeed, a great deal of pain, most of it in the early part of the operation. But the pain seemed disconnected from me, like somebody else's pain. It bothered me, but it was also quite interesting. Can you understand that? If you've used a strong morphine-based drug yourself, perhaps you can. It does more than dull pain. It induces a state of mind. A serenity. I can understand why people get hooked on it, although "hooked" seems an awfully strong word, used most commonly, of course, by those who have never tried it.

About halfway through, the pain started to become a more personal thing. Waves of faintness washed over me. I looked longingly at the open bag of white powder, but forced myself to look away. If I went on the nod again, I'd bleed to death as surely as if I'd fainted. I counted backward from a hundred instead.

Loss of blood was the most critical factor. As a surgeon, I was vitally aware of that. Not a drop could be spilled

unnecessarily. If a patient hemorrhages during an operation in a hospital, you can give him blood. I had no such
supplies. What was lost—and by the time I had finished,
the sand beneath my leg was dark with it—was lost until
my own internal factory could resupply. I had no clamps,
no hemostats, no surgical thread.

I began the operation at exactly 12:45. I finished at
1:50, and immediately dosed myself with heroin, a bigger
dose than before. I nodded into a gray, painless world and
remained there until nearly five o'clock. When I came out
of it, the sun was nearing the western horizon, beating a
track of gold across the blue Pacific toward me. I've never
seen anything so beautiful . . . all the pain was paid for in
that one instant. An hour later I snorted a bit more, so as
to fully enjoy and appreciate the sunset.

Shortly after dark I—

I—

Wait. Haven't I told you I'd had nothing to eat *for four
days?* And that the only help I could look to in the matter
of replenishing my sapped vitality was my own body?
Above all, haven't I told you, over and over, that survival
is a business of the mind? The superior mind? I won't justify
myself by saying you would have done the same thing. First
of all, you're probably not a surgeon. Even if you knew the
mechanics of amputation, you might have botched the job
so badly you would have bled to death anyway. And even
if you had lived through the operation and the shock-
trauma, the thought might never have entered your pre-
conditioned head. Never mind. No one has to know. My last
act before leaving the island will be to destroy this book.

I was very careful.

I washed it thoroughly before I ate it.

February 7

Pain from the stump has been bad—excruciating from time to time. But I think the deep-seated itch as the healing process begins has been worse. I've been thinking this afternoon of all the patients that have babbled to me that they couldn't stand the horrible, unscratchable itch of mending flesh. And I would smile and tell them they would feel better tomorrow, privately thinking what whiners they were, what jellyfish, what ungrateful babies. Now I understand. Several times I've come close to ripping the shirt bandage off the stump and scratching at it, digging my fingers into the soft raw flesh, pulling out the rough stitches, letting the blood gout onto the sand, anything, anything, to be rid of that maddening horrible *itch*.

At those times I count backward from one hundred. And snort heroin.

I have no idea how much I've taken into my system, but I do know I've been "stoned" almost continually since the operation. It depresses hunger, you know. I'm hardly aware of being hungry at all.

There is a faint, faraway gnawing in my belly, and that's all. It could easily be ignored. I can't do that, though. Heroin has no measurable caloric value. I've been testing myself, crawling from place to place, measuring my energy. It's ebbing.

Dear God, I hope not, but . . . another operation may be necessary.

(later)

Another plane flew over. Too high to do me any good; all I could see was the contrail etching itself across the sky. I waved anyway. Waved and screamed at it. When it was gone I wept.

Getting too dark to see now. Food. I've been thinking about all kinds of food. My mother's lasagna. Garlic bread. Escargots. Lobster. Prime ribs. Peach melba. London broil. The huge slice of pound cake and the scoop of homemade vanilla ice cream they give you for dessert in Mother Crunch on First Avenue. Hot pretzels baked salmon baked Alaska baked ham with pineapple rings. Onion rings. Onion dip with potato chips cold iced tea in long long sips french fries make you smack your lips.

100, 99, 98, 97, 96, 95, 94

God God God

February 8

Another gull landed on the rockpile this morning. A huge fat one. I was sitting in the shade of my rock, what I think of as my camp, my bandaged stump propped up. I began to salivate as soon as the gull landed. Just like one of Pavlov's dogs. Drooling helplessly, like a baby. Like a baby.

I picked up a chunk of stone large enough to fit my hand nicely and began to crawl toward it. Fourth quarter. We're down by three. Third and long yardage. Pinzetti drops back to pass (Pine, I mean *Pine*). I didn't have much hope. I was sure it would fly off. But I had to try. If I could get it, a bird as plump and insolent as that one, could postpone a second operation indefinitely. I crawled toward it, my stump hitting a rock from time to time and sending stars of pain through my whole body, and waited for it to fly off.

It didn't. It just strutted back and forth, its meaty breast thrown out like some avian general reviewing troops. Every now and then it would look at me with its small, nasty black eyes and I would freeze like a stone and count backward from one hundred until it began to pace back and forth again. Every time it fluttered its wings, my stomach filled up with ice. I continued to drool. I couldn't help it. I was drooling like a baby.

I don't know how long I stalked it. An hour? Two? And the closer I got, the harder my heart pounded and the tastier that gull looked. It almost seemed to be teasing me, and I began to believe that as soon as I got in throwing range it would fly off. My arms and legs were beginning to tremble. My mouth was dry. The stump was twanging viciously. I think now that I must have been having withdrawal pains. But so soon? I've been using the stuff less than a week!

Never mind. I need it. There's plenty left, plenty. If I have to take the cure later on when I get back to the States, I'll check into the best clinic in California and do it with a smile. That's not the problem right now, is it?

When I did get in range, I didn't want to throw the rock. I became insanely sure that I would miss, probably by feet. I had to get closer. So I continued to crawl up the rockpile, my head thrown back, the sweat pouring off my wasted, scarecrow body. My teeth have begun to rot, did I tell you that? If I were a superstitious man, I'd say it was because I ate—

Ha! We know better, don't we?

I stopped again. I was much closer to it than I had been to either of the other gulls. I still couldn't bring myself to commit. I clutched the rock until my fingers ached and still I couldn't throw it. Because I knew exactly what it would mean if I missed.

I don't care if I use all the merchandise! I'll sue the ass off them! I'll be in clover for the rest of my life! *My long long life!*

I think I would have crawled right up to it without throwing if it hadn't finally taken wing. I would have crept up and strangled it. But it spread its wings and took off. I screamed at it and reared up on my knees and threw my rock with all my strength. And I hit it!

The bird gave a strangled squawk and fell back on the other side of the rockpile. Gibbering and laughing, unmindful now of striking the stump or opening the wound, I crawled over the top and to the other side. I lost my balance and banged my head. I didn't even notice it, not then, although it has raised a pretty nasty lump. All I could think of was the bird and how I had hit it, fantastic luck, even on the wing I had hit it!

It was flopping down toward the beach on the other side, one wing broken, its underbody red with blood. I crawled as fast as I could, but it crawled faster yet. Race of the cripples! Ha! Ha! I might have gotten it—I was closing the distance—except for my hands. I have to take good care of my hands. I may need them again. In spite of my care, the palms were scraped by the time we reached the narrow shingle of beach, and I'd shattered the face of my Pulsar watch against a rough spine of rock.

The gull flopped into the water, squawking noisomely, and I clutched at it. I got a handful of tailfeathers, which came off in my fist. Then I fell in, inhaling water, snorting and choking.

I crawled in further. I even tried to swim after it. The bandage came off my stump. I began to go under. I just managed to get back to the beach, shaking with exhaustion, racked with pain, weeping and screaming, cursing the gull. It floated there for a long time, always further and further out. I seem to remember begging it to come back at one point. But when it went out over the reef, I think it was dead.

It isn't fair.

It took me almost an hour to crawl back around to my camp. I've snorted a large amount of heroin, but even so I'm bitterly angry at the gull. If I wasn't going to get it, why did it have to tease me so? Why didn't it just fly off?

February 9

I've amputated my left foot and have bandaged it with my pants. Strange. All through the operation I was drooling. Drooooling. Just like when I saw the gull. Drooling helplessly. But I made myself wait until after dark. I just counted backward from one hundred . . . twenty or thirty times! Ha! Ha!

Then . . .

I kept telling myself: Cold roast beef. Cold roast beef. Cold roast beef.

February 11 (?)

Rain the last two days. And high winds. I managed to move some rocks from the central pile, enough to make a hole I could crawl into. Found one small spider. Pinched it between my fingers before he could get away and ate him up. Very nice. Juicy. Thought to myself that the rocks over me might fall and bury me alive. Didn't care.

Spent the whole storm stoned. Maybe it rained three days instead of two. Or only one. But I think it got dark twice. I love to nod off. No pain or itching then. I know I'm going to survive this. It can't be a person can go through something like this for nothing.

There was a priest at Holy Family when I was a kid, a little runty guy, and he used to love to talk about hell and mortal sins. He had a real hobbyhorse on them. You can't get back from a mortal sin, that was his view. I dreamed about him last night, Father Hailley in his black bathrobe, and his whiskey nose, shaking his finger at me and saying, "Shame on you, Richard Pinzetti . . . a mortal sin . . . damt to hell, boy . . . damt to hell . . ."

I laughed at him. If this place isn't hell, what is? And the only mortal sin is giving up.

Half of the time I'm delirious; the rest of the time my stumps itch and the dampness makes them ache horribly.

But I won't give up. I swear. Not for nothing. Not all this for nothing.

February 12

Sun is out again, a beautiful day. I hope they're freezing their asses off in the neighborhood.

It's been a good day for me, as good as any day gets on this island. The fever I had while it was storming seems to have dropped. I was weak and shivering when I crawled out of my burrow, but after lying on the hot sand in the sunshine for two or three hours, I began to feel almost human again.

Crawled around to the south side and found several pieces of driftwood cast up by the storm, including several boards from my lifeboat. There was kelp and seaweed on some of the boards. I ate it. Tasted awful. Like eating a vinyl shower curtain. But I felt so much stronger this afternoon.

I pulled the wood up as far as I could so it would dry. I've still got a whole tube of waterproof matches. The wood will make a signal fire if someone comes soon. A cooking fire if not. I'm going to snort up now.

February 13

Found a crab. Killed it and roasted it over a small fire. Tonight I could almost believe in God again.

Feb 14

I just noticed this morning that the storm washed away most of the rocks in my HELP sign. But the storm ended . . . three days ago? Have I really been that stoned? I'll have to watch it, cut down the dosage. What if a ship went by while I was nodding?

I made the letters again, but it took me most of the day and now I'm exhausted. Looked for a crab where I found the other, but nothing. Cut my hands on several of the rocks I used for the sign, but disinfected them promptly with iodine in spite of my weariness. Have to take care of my hands. No matter what.

Feb 15

A gull landed on the tip of the rockpile today. Flew away before I could get in range. I wished it into hell, where it could peck out Father Hailley's bloodshot little eyes through eternity.

Ha! Ha!
Ha! Ha!
Ha

Feb 17 (?)

Took off my right leg at the knee, but lost a lot of blood. Pain excruciating in spite of heroin. Shock-trauma would have killed a lesser man. Let me answer with a question: How badly does the patient want to survive? *How badly does the patient want to live?*

Hands trembling. If they are betraying me, I'm through. They have no right to betray me. No right at all. I've taken care of them all their lives. Pampered them. They better not. Or they'll be sorry.

At least I'm not hungry.

One of the boards from the lifeboat had split down the middle. One end came to a point. I used that. I was drooling but I made myself wait. And then I got thinking of . . . oh, barbecues we used to have. That place Will Hammersmith had on Long Island, with a barbecue pit big enough to roast a whole pig in. We'd be sitting on the porch in the dusk with big drinks in our hands, talking about surgical techniques or golf scores or something. And the breeze would pick up and drift the sweet smell of roasting pork over to us. Judas Iscariot, the sweet smell of roasting pork.

Feb ?

Took the other leg at the knee. Sleepy all day. "Doctor was this operation necessary?" Haha. Shaky hands, like an old man. Hate them. Blood under the fingernails. Scabs. Remember that model in med school with the glass belly? I feel like that. Only I don't want to look. No way no how. I remember Dom used to say that. Waltz up to you on the street corner in his Hiway Outlaws club jacket. You'd say Dom how'd you make out with her? And Dom would say no way no how. Shee. Old Dom. I wish I'd stayed right in the neighborhood. This sucks so bad as Dom would say. haha.

But I understand, you know, that with the proper therapy, and prosthetics, I could be as good as new. I could come back here and tell people "This. Is where it. Happened."

Hahaha!

February 23 (?)

Found a dead fish. Rotten and stinking. Ate it anyway. Wanted to puke, wouldn't let myself. *I will survive.* So lovely stoned, the sunsets.

February

Don't dare but have to. But how can I tie off the femoral artery that high up? It's as big as a fucking turnpike up there.

Must, somehow. I've marked across the top of the thigh, the part that is still meaty. I made the mark with this pencil.

I wish I could stop drooling.

Fe

You . . . deserve . . . a break today . . . sooo . . . get up and get away . . . to McDonald's . . . two all-beef patties . . . special sauce . . . lettuce . . . pickles . . . onions . . . on a . . . sesame seed bun . . .

Dee . . . deedee . . . dundadee . . .

Febba

Looked at my face in the water today. Nothing but a skin-covered skull. Am I insane yet? I must be. I'm a monster now, a freak. Nothing left below the groin. Just a freak. A head attached to a torso dragging itself along the sand by the elbows. A crab. A *stoned* crab. Isn't that what they call themselves now? Hey man I'm just a poor stoned crab can you spare me a dime.

HAHAHAHA

They say you are what you eat and if so I HAVEN'T CHANGED A BIT! Dear God shock-trauma shock-trauma THERE IS NO SUCH THING AS SHOCK-TRAUMA

HA

Fe/40?

Dreaming about my father. When he was drunk he lost all his English. Not that he had anything worth saying anyway. Fucking dipstick. I was so glad to get out of your house Daddy you fucking greaseball dipstick nothing cipher zilcho zero. I knew I'd made it. I walked away from you, didn't I? I walked on my hands.

But there's nothing left for them to cut off. Yesterday I . . . my earlobes

left hands washes the right don't let your left hand know what your right hands doing one potato two potato three potato four we got a refrigerator with a store-more door hahaha.

Who cares. this hand or that. good food good meat good God let's eat.

lady fingers they taste just like lady fingers

FROM ALBATROSS

DEBORAH SCALING KILEY AND MEG NOONAN

Deborah Scaling Kiley was part of the crew of the fifty-eight-foot yacht Trashman *when it hit heavy seas in the Atlantic and went down. Though five shared the inflatable dinghy after the tragedy, only two survived by the time they were spotted by a Russian freighter. Here is her account of losing the captain of the* Trashman.

"I need more fucking room!" Somebody was screaming at me and hitting me. I opened my eyes. Mark.

"You're taking up too much room." He kicked me again. "She's dying. I have to get away from her."

I felt the dinghy rocking. I tried to get oriented. It was dark and my teeth were chattering. I couldn't feel my feet at all. Seaweed was tangled around my body, and I had an awful taste in my mouth. Meg was moaning and

Mark was yelling at me and I had been sleeping and I couldn't get ahold of where I was or what was happening.

"Brad?" I called, reaching out. He wasn't there. I shouted for him again and pulled myself out from under the bow cover. I tried to focus in the blackness. I could make out John and Meg, huddled together, and Brad, sitting on the starboard side of the dinghy.

"What are you doing?" I asked.

"I'm just giving Mark some more room so he'll be quiet," he said flatly, never taking his eyes off John and Meg. John had his arms around Meg, and the two of them were rocking back and forth. Meg moaned, John rocked. Meg moaned, John rocked. I wanted to look away, but I kept staring.

"I need water," John said. "I need water."

"My ankle's cut," Mark said, clutching his foot. "It's infected. I know it's infected. What if I get the same disease she has? I have to move, I need more bloody room. Look at her, she's gonna die. She's gonna die. I have to get away from her. She's gonna die."

I knew I should try to shut him up, but I said nothing. I didn't have the energy. Maybe Meg couldn't even hear him now. What was the point of trying to stop anyone from doing anything? Mark was screaming and John was rocking and Meg was moaning and Brad was just sitting there staring at nothing. The stench and the filth and the rot and the emptiness—it was the darkest, darkest nightmare.

If only it would rain, I thought. A warm rain, soft and steady. Everything would be better if I could feel the rain on my skin, let it run over me, wash it all away. I started reciting the Twenty-third Psalm—the Lord is my shepherd, I shall not want. I wanted to see if I could remember the words, the simple, soothing words—words that fell like raindrops, leaving soft circles of hope.

Sometime later, everyone was quiet again. Brad was up on the side. Meg, John, and Mark all seemed to be asleep. The dinghy moved from wave to wave, my teeth chattered, the wind blew. Silence is so loud, I thought.

"Brad," I whispered.

"What?" I had startled him.

"Why don't you come down here and get some sleep? Aren't you freezing up there?"

"I'm okay," he said and looked away.

"Please, Brad. I need you down here."

He didn't move. I was so afraid he would fall asleep and then drop off the Zodiac if we hit a wave.

"Please. I'd just feel a lot better if you were down here. It's not very safe sitting up there."

Without a word he lowered himself down next to me. We huddled together and I felt better. I allowed myself the great luxury of sleep.

Meg was moaning again. Mark was whining about not having any room. John was babbling about water. They were driving me insane, the three of them. If Meg would just shut up—my God, how could I be angry at Meg for moaning? How could I be so heartless? I started in on the whys again. Why this? Why now? Why me? I was imperfect. I had done some not-so-great things in my life. But this? This was my punishment? I felt I was supposed to learn something from this ordeal, some key, something magical and pure. And when I found it I would take it . . . Shit, where would I take it now? I dozed off again.

"Debbie," Brad was whispering. It was still dark. "Yeah?"

"Listen. What do you think they're doing?"

I lifted my head and strained to see the others. I could see two forms—John and Mark—leaning over the stern.

"What are they doing?" Brad said again.

I couldn't hear what they were saying. I felt a rush of panic. Were they doing something to the boat? Or to Meg? No. Meg was all right. She was sitting with her head on her knees, asleep. I could hear the two guys splashing water. Then I understood. They were drinking seawater. I was stunned. How could they be so stupid?

"They're drinking it," I said to Brad. "Should we stop them?"

"It's probably too late," Brad said.

I felt such sadness listening to them. They had given in, they had lost control. I knew that drinking sea water was a terrible mistake—I remembered hearing that you should drink your own urine first. I didn't know what would happen to them. Would they go mad, or had they already? Would they die? Would they try to do something to the rest of us?

"Brad. Promise me you won't drink it," I whispered.

He didn't answer. That scared me even more. I dropped my head back down, and the water in the dinghy sloshed up around my mouth. I imagined myself opening my mouth and drinking; hanging my head over the side and letting the ocean flow in. How would it taste? How would it feel?

Dawn broke, and for the first time since the sinking it looked as if we might see the sun. The clouds were breaking up. The thought of feeling the sun on my skin gave me a renewed sense of hope. Maybe the Coast Guard was coming after all. Of course they were. So they had some problems getting to us, okay. But now the sea was calmer and there was no reason they couldn't get to us today—hell, maybe they'll be here within the hour.

Don't be a fool, Debbie. If the Coast Guard was looking for us they would have found us by now. They aren't coming; that's all there is to it. "God helps those who help themselves," my grandmother Queenie used to say. I will help myself, I thought. All I have is myself. I will not fall apart.

Brad ducked out from under the bow. Mark and John stirred, and Meg groaned. Her bad leg looked even worse; the gruesome red streaks had become wider, and now they ran all the way up, disappearing under her shirt.

"They'll come today," John said.

"They better. Look at my ankle," Mark said. The infection in his ankle had spread down to his foot. "What am I going to do?"

"The sun is over there," Brad said slowly, "so it seems like the wind is northerly and the seas are from the northeast. We should be drifting toward land. We might just wash ashore sometime in the next couple of days."

"South Carolina or Georgia, maybe," Mark said.

I was cheered by that image, washing up on a low barrier beach.

"What do we do when we get there?" Meg asked. "Go to the Coast Guard station?"

"Hell, no," John said. "I'm flying home. Those bastards left us out there. Fuck 'em."

"You know I hate to fly," Meg said. "Let's just go to the Coast Guard station and let them take care of us."

John shrugged. Then he sat up straight and pointed.

"I see land," he said.

We all turned and looked.

"Right there, man. See it? It's right in front of us!"

I strained to see it, but I could see nothing but water.

"I think you're seeing things, bro," Brad said.

John slumped against the stern and sighed.

"So where would we fly, anyway?" Meg asked John.

"Probably to Portland. We'd go to my mom's."

"I don't want to fly there. I want to go to the Coast Guard station. I can't get on a plane like this. I might give someone this disease."

"What are you talking about?" I said to Meg.

"This thing I have. I don't want to give it to anyone."

"That's not a disease, Meg," I said. "It's blood poisoning. Nobody can catch it."

"I don't want to fly!" Meg said. Tears were spilling down her face. "John knows I can't fly. Please don't make me."

John put his arm around her.

"It's okay, Meg," I said. "You don't have to fly. When we get there we'll put you on a train or rent a car or something . . ."

"Yeah, we'll do whatever you want," Brad said.

She continued to sob.

"Christ, Meg, shut up," Mark said and kicked at her.

She wailed harder.

John didn't seem to notice. "We won't have to fly. We'll just get the car," he said. "We're right off Falmouth, so we'll just drive to the hospital where my mom works. She'll take care of us."

I couldn't believe John would tell Meg such a cruel lie. Then I realized that he believed what he was saying.

"We're not off Falmouth," Brad said. "We're out in the middle of the Atlantic Ocean somewhere. We're nowhere near Falmouth."

"Bullshit. It's right over there," John said with conviction.

"What the hell is wrong with you?" Mark said.

"Nothing's wrong with me," John said angrily.

Brad suggested Meg move up to the bow for a while. He thought if she tucked her legs up under the bow no one would be able to bump them.

"Deb and I can sit on the sides. And Mark can scoot to the back and you could stretch out a little more."

I nodded in agreement, though I wasn't happy about having to give up my spot.

"What about my foot?" Mark whined. "I need to stretch out, too. I want to get up there."

"Meg's in worse shape than you, Mark," I said.

"I'm going to sit up there next," Mark said.

John and Brad helped Meg slide up to the bow. John moved as if he were in a trance. His eyes were fixed and his movements slow and unnaturally deliberate. I sat up on the side for a few minutes, but I was too exposed to the wind, so I dropped down to the floor and leaned against the stern. Nobody said anything. I searched what I thought was the western horizon, looking for land, for anything.

"Quit it," I heard Meg say. "You're kicking me."

"I'm not kicking you," John replied.

"Cut it out."

"Quit bitching. All you do is bitch," John snapped.

"Where are my fucking cigarettes?" Mark suddenly shouted. His eyes were wide and wild-looking, and he was digging through the small mound of rotting seaweed in the bottom of the dinghy. "Who took them?"

"What are you talking about?" Brad said. "You don't have any cigarettes."

"What the fuck? You took them, didn't you?" Mark said to Brad.

"There aren't any cigarettes. Even if you did have some they would be sopping wet by now."

"I have cigarettes," Mark said slowly.

"Where'd you get them?" Brad asked.

"I just went to the Seven-Eleven and I bought beer and cigarettes. And I want to know who took them."

I stared at Mark in disbelief. He was out of his mind. Totally gone.

"Mark," I said, thinking I might be able to reason him back to reality. "If you did just go to the Seven-Eleven, then why the hell did you come back?"

Mark sat in the rotten seaweed and stared down at his palms. He looked at Brad, then at me, then at Brad again. He blinked fast, as if he was trying to focus, then pulled his shoulders up toward his ears and winced and closed his eyes. He tried to speak, but the words seemed to get jammed up in his mouth.

"Wh-where a-are m-m-mmy bl-bl-oody cig-a-re-rettes?" he stammered and resumed pawing through the stinking weed.

Then Meg was shouting at John again and John was shouting back and Mark was ranting and I felt myself drowning in the sound of their voices, the whining, the shouting, the crying, the complaining. Why couldn't every-one just be quiet? I saw John kick Meg. He was doing it on purpose. She wailed and he kicked her again.

"Stop it, John," I said. "Don't you think she's in enough pain without you making it worse? Leave her alone."

John continued to jostle Meg. Meg continued to scream and cry. Mark was still trying to find his cigarettes. Finally Meg said she didn't want to be next to John any-more, so Brad and I helped her back to the stern. Mark immediately said it was his turn in the bow. While Brad and I were easing Meg back into position, I heard a strange noise. I turned in time to see John at the bow ripping off the rubber patch that secured the painter to the dinghy.

Brad and I hollered at John, but he pulled it off cleanly and threw it into the water before falling back against the stern. My knees buckled. I knew that in the next second the air would come hissing out of the Zodiac. I crawled forward, and Mark shouted, "Where the hell do you think you're going! It's my turn!"

I fell onto the bow and ran my hand over the rub-ber where the patch had been. Maybe I could plug the hole somehow, maybe there was a chance. To my relief, it seemed to be intact. There was no hole, no escaping air, no damage at all.

"Are you trying to kill us all?" I said to John, but I could see that he had no idea what he had done. His eyes were flat and dull. He was a million miles away. I knew he was in big trouble—maybe it was hypothermia or maybe the effects of drinking salt water.

Mark pushed me aside so he could claim his spot in the bow. I moved back to the spot where Mark had been sitting. Meg sat crumpled in the corner whimpering. I followed John's every move, terrified of what he might do next. I spotted the air valves in the stern. Please don't notice them, I said to myself. I willed John to look the other way.

I had to stretch. My legs were cramped and stiff. Mark had become engrossed again in searching for his phantom cigarettes, so I didn't think he would notice if I stretched my legs out straight just for a minute. As I unfolded them I saw how swollen they had become. The saltwater sores had grown, too. My skin looked as if someone had stubbed out big cigars on it. Some of the sores were red and hot and oozing. I wondered whether I would be able to walk once we got back to land.

Suddenly I felt a searing bolt of pain shoot up my left leg, through my groin, and up to the top of my head. I screamed and flew forward and slammed my fist into Mark's back.

"Bastard!" He had twisted my wounded toe. Blood spurted from it.

"Why can't you leave everyone alone?" Brad shouted.

"She's in my place," he said. "I want it back."

He pushed me out of the way and crawled to the

port side. Brad and I moved back to the bow. I kept my eyes on Mark and John.

"Hey," Mark said to John. "Want a smoke?"

"Sure," John said. "Got any?"

"Under the seaweed. Up there." Mark moved toward the bow again.

"Mark. Listen to me, man. There aren't any smokes or beer or anything up here," Brad said. "We're out in the middle of the ocean."

"I got some sandwiches," John said. "You want one?"

It was pure horror, watching Mark and John carry on about their cigarettes and their sandwiches. They seemed to genuinely believe they had just been to the store and picked up supplies—as if they were just out on a day sail. They had both moved, simultaneously, into some other reality.

"Okay, where are they? John hollered, picking up seaweed and tossing it overboard. "I know they were here."

"Where are my bloody fags?" Mark asked me. "I know you took them." He started to come at me, but Brad put up his hand to protect me.

"She doesn't have them, Mark," Brad shouted. "Leave her alone." Mark stared at us, then collapsed back against the side of the Zodiac. John slid down next to him, looking confused.

I slept. It was a tortured, fitful sleep, full of voices and cries. I awoke with the feeling that a shadow had just crossed my face. I sat up. Everyone was sleeping. It was dusk again. The clouds that had blocked the sun for so long were finally gone. I knew that this night was going to be colder than the others—the clouds, at least, had held in some warmth. Now I knew for sure where the west was, and I tried to convince myself that we were drifting in that direction. I watched the sky as we rode the swells and slid westward, toward land, toward life.

Meg's moans startled me. Had I been asleep again? The eastern sky was indigo-black now and pricked with a few bright stars. The western horizon still held some light.

"Meg," I said quietly. I didn't want to wake John and Mark.

She moaned again

"Meg. Do you want to try sitting up here? You could stretch your legs out again."

"I want to sit up on the side," she said, and John's eyes opened.

"What?" John said with alarm.

"It's okay, John," I said. "Meg just needs to stretch out. She wants to get up on the side."

John immediately started to help Meg lift herself up. I was relieved to see him respond to her. Maybe he was okay. Whatever it was that had made him so irrational had been temporary.

Once Meg was up on the side, she said, "I've been thinking about it, and I've decided that if the Coast Guard wants to fly us to your mom's, it's okay with me. I just want to go home."

"We'll go straight home," John said.

"I don't normally like to fly, but—"

"I know, but just this once—"

"Yeah. I mean, it's probably the best way to go."

Brad woke up and listened to the two of them talk.

Then Mark stirred. I felt myself go rigid with apprehension.

"See, that's west," Brad said. "We're definitely heading toward land. We have to wash up on shore eventually."

"When do you think?" Meg asked.

"Tomorrow, maybe the day after."

"I can't wait to see the look on the faces of those Coast Guard guys when we show up on their bloody doorstep," Mark said.

"Do you think they'll fly us in a private plane or a commercial plane?" Meg said.

"I can't believe they just left us out here," I said. "They never do that."

"What do you think, John, private or commercial plane?"

"Quit talking about planes," John said sharply. "I'm sick of hearing you talk about planes."

"I was just wondering—"

"We're not going on a plane. That would be stupid. I'm just going to go get the car."

"There isn't any car, John," I said.

"We're just off Falmouth. I know right where the car is. I'll go get it," he said. "You guys bring the boat in and I'll get the car. Then we can unload."

He sounded so sure, I had to fight to keep from being sucked into the fantasy. Was he right? Were we just off Falmouth? Then why . . . no, that wasn't right. It couldn't be. I closed my eyes and shook my head, trying to clear it, trying to stay focused on what was real. When I looked up again I saw John lowering himself over the side of the Zodiac.

"What are you doing?" Brad and I both hollered.

"I'll be back in a few," John said matter-of-factly.

"What about the sharks?" Mark asked.

"John, if you leave this dinghy we may not be able to get you back in," I said. "It's almost dark. Why don't you just come on back in now." I was trying to keep my voice even and calm. I had no idea what John was going to do, what might set him off. Was he just trying to get warm? Did he really think we were close to home?

"I can't take this anymore," he said. "I'm going to go get the car."

Brad and I looked at each other. John's hands slid away from the gunwale and he began to swim. He stopped for a minute, treading water and looking back at us. I thought he might be playing a sick joke. Meg was begging him to come back, pleading with one of us to go get him.

"Should I go after him?" Brad said to me.

I didn't know. I couldn't think. Was he really going to just swim away?

"Should I?" Brad sounded panicky, John turned and started stroking away from the Zodiac.

"John!" Meg cried.

"You can't go after him, Brad," I said. There was almost no light left in the sky. It would be impossible to force him back to the dinghy—and it would be suicidal to try. What if Brad went in and we lost him, too? We all watched John swim. Meg, her hands over her mouth, was shaking her head slowly and sobbing. John went up over a swell, disappeared, then reappeared farther off.

"Should I go?" Brad asked again.

"Don't go after him," Meg said quietly. "He's gone."

We rode up a big swell, and I saw John's head again, dark against the dark sea. And then we heard a terrible, gut-twisting scream.

"My God, he's calling me," Meg said and dissolved into tears.

We scanned the black water hoping for another glimpse of him. But Meg was right. John was gone.

*In 1955, while working as a journalist, Gabriel
García Márquez interviewed one of the survivors
from a Colombian destroyer that had lost several
crewmembers when they were washed overboard.
Though the story reads almost like the author's
fiction, this excerpt was part of the series of articles
describing the sailor's ordeal that García Márquez
wrote for a Bogotá newspaper.*

Fighting Off the Sharks for a Fish

The thought that for seven days I had been drifting farther
out to sea rather than nearing land crushed my resolve to
keep on struggling. But when you feel close to death, your
instinct for self-preservation grows stronger. For several
reasons, that day was very different from the previous days:
the sea was dark and calm; the sun, warm and tranquil,

hugged my body; a gentle breeze guided the raft along; even my sunburn felt a bit better.

The fish were different, too. From very early on they had escorted the raft, swimming near the surface. And I could see them clearly: blue fish, gray-brown ones, red ones. There were fish of every color, all shapes and sizes. It seemed as if the raft were floating in an aquarium.

I don't know whether, after seven days without food and adrift at sea, one becomes accustomed to living that way. I think so. The hopelessness of the previous day was replaced by a mellow resignation devoid of emotion. I was sure that everything was different, that the sea and the sky were no longer hostile, and that the fish accompanying me on my journey were my friends. My old acquaintances of seven days.

That morning I wasn't thinking about reaching any destination. I was certain that the raft had arrived in a region where there were no ships, where even sea gulls could go astray.

I thought, however, that after seven days adrift I would become accustomed to the sea, to my anxious way of life, without having to spur my imagination in order to survive. After all, I had endured a week of harsh winds and waves. Why wouldn't it be possible to live on the raft indefinitely? The fish swam near the surface; the sea was clear and calm. There were so many lovely, tempting fish around the raft it looked as if I could grab them with my hands. Not a shark was in sight. Confidently I put my hand in the water and tried to seize a round fish, a bright blue one about twenty centimeters long. It was as if I had flung a stone:

all the fish fled instantly, momentarily churning up the water. Then slowly they came back to the surface.

You have to be crafty to fish with your hand, I thought. Underwater, the hand didn't have as much strength or agility. I chose one fish from the bunch. I tried to grab it. And in fact I did. But I felt it slip through my fingers with disconcerting speed and nimbleness. I waited patiently, not pressuring myself, just trying to catch a fish. I wasn't thinking about the shark which might be out there, waiting until I put my arm in up to the elbow so he could make off with it in one sure bite. I kept busy trying to catch fish until a little after ten o'clock. But it was useless. They nibbled at my fingers, gently at first, as when they nibble at bait. Then a little harder. A smooth silver fish about a foot and a half long, with minute, sharp teeth, tore the skin off my thumb. Then I realized that the nibbles of the other fish hadn't been harmless: all my fingers had small bleeding cuts.

Shark in the raft!

I don't know if it was the blood from my fingers, but in an instant there was a riot of sharks around the raft. I had never seen so many. I had never seen them so voracious. They leaped like dolphins, chasing the fish and devouring them. Terrified, I sat in the middle of the raft and watched the massacre.

The next thing happened so quickly that I didn't realize just when it was that the shark leaped out of the water, thrashing its tail violently, and the raft, tottering, sank beneath the gleaming foam. In the midst of the huge, glittering wave that crashed over the side there was a metallic flash. Instinctively I grabbed an oar and prepared to strike a deathblow. But then I saw the enormous fin, and I realized what had happened. Chased by the shark, a brilliant green fish, almost half a meter long, had leaped into the raft. With all my strength I walloped it on the head with my oar.

Killing a fish inside a raft isn't easy. The vessel tottered with each blow; it might have turned over. It was a perilous moment. I needed all my strength and all my wits about me. If I struck out blindly, the raft would turn over and I would plunge into a sea full of hungry sharks. If I didn't aim carefully, my quarry would escape. I stood between life and death. I would either end up in the gullet of a shark or get four pounds of fresh fish to appease the hunger of seven days.

I braced myself on the gunwale and struck the second blow. I felt the wooden oar drive into the fish's skull. The raft bounced. The sharks shuddered below. I pressed myself firmly against the side. When the raft stabilized, the fish was still alive.

In agony, a fish can jump higher and farther than it otherwise can. I knew the third blow had to be a sure one or I would lose my prey forever.

After a lunge at the fish, I found myself sitting on the floor, where I thought I had a better chance of grabbing it. If necessary, I would have captured it with my feet, between my knees, or in my teeth. I anchored myself to the floor. Trying not to make a mistake and convinced that my life depended on my next blow, I swung the oar with all my strength. The fish stopped moving and a thread of dark blood tinted the water inside the raft.

I could smell the blood, and the sharks sensed it, too. Suddenly, with four pounds of fish within my grasp, I felt uncontrollable terror: driven wild by the scent of blood, the sharks hurled themselves with all their strength against the bottom of the raft. The raft shook. I realized that it could turn over in an instant. I could be torn to pieces by the three rows of steel teeth in the jaws of each shark.

But the pressure of hunger was greater than anything else. I squeezed the fish between my legs and, staggering, began the difficult job of balancing the raft each time it suffered another assault by the sharks. That went on for several minutes. Whenever the raft stabilized, I threw the bloody water overboard. Little by little the water cleared and the beasts calmed down. But I had to be careful: a terrifyingly huge shark fin—the biggest I had ever seen— protruded more than a meter above the water's surface. The shark was swimming peacefully, but I knew that if it caught the scent of blood it would give a shudder that could capsize the raft. With extreme caution I began to try to pull my fish apart.

A creature that's half a meter long is protected by a hard crust of scales: if you try to pull them off, you find that they adhere to the flesh like armor plating. I had no sharp instruments. I tried to shave off the scales with my keys, but they wouldn't budge. Meanwhile, it occurred to me that I had never seen a fish like this one: it was deep green and thickly scaled. From when I was little, I had associated the color green with poison. Incredibly, although my stomach was throbbing painfully at the prospect of even a mouthful of fresh fish, I had trouble deciding whether or not that strange creature might be poisonous.

My poor body

Hunger is bearable when you have no hope of food. But it was never so insistent as when I was trying to slash that shiny green flesh with my keys.

After a few minutes, I realized I would have to use more violent methods if I wanted to eat my victim. I stood up, stepped hard on its tail, and stuck the oar handle into one of its gills. I saw that the fish wasn't dead yet. I hit it on the head again. Then I tried to tear off the hard protective plates that covered the gills. I couldn't tell whether the blood streaming over my fingers was from the fish or from me; my hands were covered with wounds and my fingertips were raw.

The scent of blood once again stirred the sharks' hunger. It seems unbelievable but, furious at the hungry beasts and disgusted by the sight of the bloody fish, I was on the point of throwing it to the sharks, as I had done with the sea gull. I felt utterly frustrated and helpless at the sight of the solid, impenetrable body of the fish.

I examined it meticulously for soft spots. Finally I found a slit between the gills and with my finger I began to pull out the entrails. The innards of a fish are soft and without substance. It is said that if you strike a hard blow to a shark's tail the stomach and intestines fall out of its mouth. In Cartagena, I had seen sharks hanging by their tails, with huge thick masses of dark innards oozing from their mouths.

Luckily the entrails of my fish were as soft as those of the sharks. It didn't take long to remove them with my finger. It was a female: among the entrails I found a string of eggs. When it was completely gutted I took the first bite. I couldn't break through the crust of scales. But on the second try, with renewed strength, I bit down desperately, until my jaw ached. Then I managed to tear off the first mouthful and began to chew the cold, tough flesh.

I chewed with disgust. I had always found the odor of raw fish repulsive, but the flavor is even more repugnant. It tastes vaguely like raw palm, but oilier and less palatable. I couldn't imagine that anyone had ever eaten a live fish, but as I chewed the first food that had reached my lips in seven days, I had the awful certainty that I was in fact eating one.

After the first piece, I felt better immediately. I took a second bite and chewed again. A moment before, I had thought I could eat a whole shark. But now I felt full after the second mouthful. The terrible hunger of seven days was appeased in an instant. I was strong again, as on the first day.

I now know that raw fish slakes your thirst. I hadn't known it before, but I realized that the fish had appeased not only my hunger but my thirst as well. I was sated and optimistic. I still had food for a long time, since I had taken only two small bites of a creature half a meter long.

I decided to wrap the fish in my shirt and store it in the bottom of the raft to keep it fresh. But first I had to wash it. Absentmindedly I held it by the tail and dunked it once over the side. But blood had coagulated between the scales. It would have to be scrubbed. Naïvely I submerged it again. And that was when I felt the charge of the violent thrust of the shark's jaws. I hung on to the tail of the fish with all the strength I had. The beast's lunge upset my balance. I was thrown against the side of the raft but I held on to my food supply; I clung to it like a savage. In that fraction of a second, it didn't occur to me that with another bite the shark could have ripped my arm off at the shoulder. I kept pulling with all my strength, but now there was nothing in my hands. The shark had made off with my prey. Infuriated, rabid with frustration, I grabbed an oar and delivered a tremendous blow to the shark's head when it passed by the side of the raft. The beast leaped; it twisted furiously and with one clean, savage bite splintered the oar and swallowed half of it.

AND NEVER COME UP
JOHN BIGUENET

Was there a story?

Yes, there was always a story.

Did you write this one down?

I've written them all down.

Will you read it to me?

It wasn't really his story. I thought it was. I thought it had something to do with him—or one of his shipmates, at least. That it had happened on a boat he knew. But then I was reading to my son one night, and there it was in this book of sea stories.

Exactly the same?

No, just the idea. All the details were different.

Stories get passed on. Maybe your father heard it somewhere.

Maybe. But he made me believe it was no story. I thought it was true.

Why?

Because of what he said after he told it to me.
Read it to me. Please.
If you like.

The freighter was three days out of New Orleans on its run to Panama when the wife and daughter of the ship's captain both succumbed, in the space of a few hours, to a fever from which they had suffered since their first day at sea.

As the bodies of the handsome woman and the little girl were wound in canvas for burial, old salts, shaking their heads, repeated to the younger hands the ancient injunction against sailing with women. 'It's a terrible shame, but we're lucky it weren't worse,' the bosun confided to the third mate, who had brought the sorrowful news to the bridge.

The captain, with twenty years' experience of the vagaries of the sea, was not so bold a man as to have been indifferent to the superstition. In fact, he had for a year denied the repeated entreaties of his daughter to take her with him on a voyage. Only as a special birthday present to this child whom he adored without measure had he relented. His wife, delighted that at least once in her life she would not have to bid farewell to her beloved husband from the edge of a dock, spurred him to live up to his promise.

And so, on 2 September, with the assurance of the harbour master that the Gulf threatened no hurricane at the moment, the captain ushered aboard his ship the child and her mother. Having slipped its moorings, the freighter nosed down the Mississippi under the command of a river pilot. At the mouth of the river, the pilot disembarked, remarking to his fellows when he had returned to Pilot-town on the captain who had taken the whole family to sea. 'He some crazy, huh?' the pilot's father observed.

Already the woman and her child were faint with their illness. 'It's to be expected,' the captain told them, and he tried to comfort them with tales of his own sea-sickness on his first trip out. But the onset of fever late that afternoon alarmed him; they were not seasick.

The ship, of course, had no doctor, but the second mate did what he could to ease their discomfort. When they grew too weak to swallow the aspirins he had taken from the medicine locker, he crushed the pills beneath his thumb in the bowl of a spoon and added a few drops of water so they might drink the medicine. But their decline was so steady and seemed to him so certain that he had shaken his head over them a good day before they finally died.

The captain, having seen his share of death in the war, trembled but held his composure as his first officer read from his Kingspoint manual the liturgy for burial at sea. The crew, unpracticed in this drill, stumbled in sliding the bodies over the side. The ship's navigator, as required by maritime custom, shot the sun and fixed the location of the burial, noting it on the ship's chart and conveying it to the captain for entry in the log.

The remainder of the voyage was uneventful. One of the sailors got into a bit of trouble on shore leave, but the local authorities were glad to release him to the custody of an officer of the ship.

The freighter, now laden with coffee, retraced its route back to New Orleans. Two days out of Panama, in the middle of the third watch, an officer called the captain to the bridge.

Fifty yards off the starboard bow, the water rose up in the shape, vaguely, of two figures—one somewhat taller than the other. The captain dropped his binoculars. 'Sir,' the navigator nearly whispered, 'we're very close to the spot, very close.'

As the ship slid past, the watery figures trembled in the bright sunlight. Finally, the watch saw the two columns of water collapse after the stern had passed them.

By the time the ship docked in New Orleans, the captain had been locked in his cabin. Orderlies from St Simon's Asylum led the man down the gangplank in restraints.

New Orleans is one of the great ports of the world. The story easily found its way to the pages of the local papers. Intrigued by the tale, the *Item* sent a photographer on the Panama run when the ship embarked a week later.

Again two watery figures rose up.

In a quiet dinner at Antoine's a few days after the photo's publication, in the face of a threatened strike by the seafarers' union, the owners of the four lines that traded with Panama agreed to re-route their ships to a more easterly course. The new route they plotted that night has been followed for the last half-century.

In all that time, no ship has passed within ten miles of the location fixed by the navigator that melancholy afternoon. Whether the sea remains calm there or whether a mother and her daughter have risen up like pillars of water each day for the last fifty years no man can say.

That's your version?

That's how I wrote it down.

But that's not how he told it to me.

No, it's not the way he told it. To be the same, it would be whispered so close to your face you could smell the breath that carried it, but in darkness so black you couldn't even see the lips that were telling it.

You're resorting to poetry again.

No, no, I'm not. That's exactly how it was, the night I heard the story. That's the absolute truth.

How is that possible? Where were you?

We were deep in the marsh, back down one of those winding canals off the ship channel. We'd been hauling in speckled trout hand over foot for better than an hour when they stopped biting. It was already nearly three, so my father tried to start the engine. He pulled on the cord till I thought he would rip the top off the motor, but it didn't even cough.

You'd been fishing?

Yeah, we had a little fourteen-foot plywood runabout my father and grandfather had built, the kind with fibreglass tape at the seams. Everybody made their own in those days. My grandfather wasn't with us, though, out in the marsh. I think maybe he was already in the hospital by then.

How old were you?

I don't know. Nine. Maybe ten.

You were just a baby.

No, I wasn't a baby. I was ten years old.

Oh, you were a baby. Ten years old.

OK, I was a baby. We had this huge outboard on the back—my father won it somehow playing pinochle—and when you leaned on the throttle, the boat just about jumped out of the water. So we called it the *Mullet.*

Mullet?

It's this little fish that jumps out of the water when something big is chasing it. You can't catch them with a hook. Their mouths are too small.

So what did your father do?

Bobbing there in our little boat, Daddy changed the spark plugs, cleaned the lines, checked the pumps, went through the whole drill. But when he popped the cover back on and tugged the cord again—nothing. We were stuck. And hunkered back in the marsh the way we were, we hadn't seen another boat in a couple of hours. It was so hot by then if your hand brushed a cleat you got burned. So there weren't many damn fools still out.

Then what did your father do?

What he always did. He pulled a bottle out of the ice chest.

But what about you? You must have been frightened, a little child like you.

There used to be a saying around here when I was a boy: 'Nobody but God can whup my daddy, and God better watch his step.' As long as Daddy was leaning back against the bow drinking Dixies, it was just another fishing trip as far as I was concerned. I knew Mama would be upset, our being late and all—and I was worried about that because I knew what would happen if she made too much of a fuss when we got home. But afraid of being stranded out in the marsh? I didn't have the slightest idea how much trouble we were in.

Your father knew what he was doing, didn't he?

Sure. In all the times we went out there, I never once saw him check a chart, and anybody'll tell you what a labyrinth those canals are. Nothing but sawgrass and water as far as you can see.

And your father had been a sailor, hadn't he?

Yeah, that's right. He was in the Merchant Marine until I was born and my mother made him come home. He sailed damn near everywhere. I don't know how many winter runs he made in the North Atlantic. The water's so cold that time of year, if you fall overboard you're dead in twenty seconds. At least, that's what he used to tell me. He dodged submarines in the Pacific during the war, took a ship through the Suez, rode out a typhoon in the South China Sea.

He must have seen some things.

He said you could walk to shore on the backs of the sharks they were so thick in Manila Bay. In fact, he lost one of his shipmates when they were unloading in the Philippines near the end of the war. The idiot got drunk and decided to go for a swim, right there where they anchored.

Didn't anybody try to stop him?

I asked my father about that once, when I was still small. That's the thing about sailors, he explained. They'll warn you off of trouble, but not a one of them will ever stop you. You want to take your boat out in weather like this? One of them will tell you, 'Might get a little wet today.' By which he means, 'If you're damn fool enough to go out on a day like this, the crabs'll be scraping the flesh from your bones at the bottom of the sea before you're done.' But nobody's going to stop you. It's your boat.

You don't have to be so grisly.

That's the way Daddy put it. He said deep down they all expected to drown sooner or later themselves, so they didn't see any point in going to a lot of trouble to keep someone from drowning sooner.

This is the kind of story your father told a ten-year-old?

Ten? He was telling me his stories before I went to school. They weren't any worse than fairy tales.

Crabs eating the flesh from your bones?

Wolves eating up grandmothers and inviting children into their beds?

So what about the man who went swimming?

My father said his buddy hadn't been in the water half a minute before a shark took his legs. But it was quiet, he said; they never saw the shark. The man rolled like a ship broaching—that's the way he always put it, and running in those Pacific convoys for two years, he saw plenty of ships broach—and the guy just bobbed there upside down for a moment or two, bloody stumps in the air, then slid under, gone.

There's really no need to—

He hated the Indian Ocean—the storms lasted so long down there they'd eat cold mess three days running because it was too rough for the cooks to make hot food. But you know what the most dangerous thing he ever did at sea? Haul molasses from the Caribbean to the East Coast.

Molasses? What's so dangerous about that?

I'll tell you how dangerous it is. Molasses carried the highest premium for hazardous cargo. That's why he did it, for the money, the bonus. And we needed the molasses for explosives, so there was a lot of demand during the war.

But what's so dangerous about it?

It's heavier than water. If a ship was hit and went down, the molasses took everything with it to the bottom of the sea. Down where the crabs were waiting.

No survivors.

None. My father was a real sailor, all right. So he knew what he was doing on the water. Of course, he told me one night when he was good and drunk that the best advice he'd gotten in a dozen years at sea was from an old sailor on the first ship he sailed, the *Howard Handstrom* I think it was. You've probably heard this saying before. 'Never learn to swim—it only prolongs the drowning.' I remember when he told me he took another swig of bourbon and then, with one eye open, swore, 'But, goddamn it, I already knew how to swim.'

So what happened to you out in the marsh?

My father and I sat there till dusk. I tried fishing some, but the water was too hot and the tide was out. Daddy kept drinking. We had some kind of cheese spread my mother had made and soda crackers, so that was our dinner. Every once in a while, Daddy would stand up on the bench and look for another boat, but nobody else was still out, and we were too far off the channel to catch a tow with the shrimp boats coming in from the Gulf. He was still in a pretty good mood, though. After he'd taken a look, he would say, 'I'd better send up a flare.' And he'd unzip his pants and take a piss, standing up on the seat. I guess it was all the beer he'd been drinking.

And what about you?

I'd kept my Dodgers baseball cap on the whole day, and, of course, we were both wearing long-sleeved shirts. But by the time the sky in the east began to turn purple, I'd had too much sun. Hot as it was and even though I was still wearing one of those big, old-fashioned life jackets, I started getting chills. Fever, I guess.

Keep a child out there all day on the water till he gets sick?

I was sick all right, but we had a bigger problem to deal with. I could already hear them lifting out of the grass before I could see them. At first I thought it was an engine. Dizzy as I was, I stood up on the bench. I was sure we were saved. I was really proud, too. Daddy had fallen asleep in the bow. I was going to be the lookout that spied a boat and saved the crew. But there weren't any boats when I looked, just small dark clouds hovering, twitching over the mud-flats. I didn't know what they were—smoke, fog? But as the roaring got louder, I looked down at my hands. They were seething with mosquitoes. It was weird, I hadn't felt a thing. Maybe it was the fever, I don't know, but I watched these bugs crawling all over themselves like it was some-body else's hands they were biting. And then very calmly, I plunged both arms into the water. With my face close to the canal, the racket from all those little wings overhead was unbelievable. I reached behind me to shake my father awake by the leg. He didn't stir. That was when I began to be afraid. So I crawled beside him, and when I got close enough to see him in the dark, his face and neck were so thick with mosquitoes he looked like he had a black beard. I tried to call out to wake him, but my mouth was full of them before I could even say his name. I choked on mosquitoes, spitting them out into the water. My coughing woke him up. By then, they were in our eyes. I think my eyelids were starting to swell shut from all the bites. The next thing I knew, Daddy had thrown me overboard and jumped in beside me.

My God.

He was spitting out the bugs even as he shouted at me. He got his shirt off and threw it over my head like a little tent. Then I felt him underwater, loosening my life jacket and working my own shirt off. I couldn't see him till he came right up in front of my face under the tent of his shirt. 'Vicious little bastards, aren't they?' he shouted even though he was just inches away. And then he said, 'Here, you put your own shirt over your head when I tell you to.' His hand brought up the sopping shirt my mother had buttoned on me that morning when it was still dark outside. I remember it had cowboys with lariats all over it. I think they were on horseback. Daddy said the first thing we had to do was tie the sleeves in knots so the mosquitoes couldn't get in. And we had to make sure that the edges of our shirts stayed in the water.

You had your life vest on?

Yeah, of course. I wasn't allowed in the boat without a life jacket. Anyway, Daddy was working in the dark on all this. It had gotten pitch black under the shirt. The brim of my baseball cap kept the fabric off my face when Daddy submerged. He had helped me slip my shirt under his own. It was a much smaller little tent. I hadn't realized how big my father was. His shirt had been huge, but I could barely keep the edges of mine in the water. In fact, it was so dark it was hard to tell where the water began. My father said to keep dipping my head under so the shirt would stay wet. 'They find you by your heat,' he whispered, as if they might hear. 'Stay wet and they won't know where you are.' That worried me. I was afraid my fever would give us away. But the water was making me feel better.

That's horrifying.

It gets worse.

Worse?

Little by little, Daddy had felt his way along the edge of the boat until he found some footing on the bottom. He could stand with his head out of the water. He had tightened the straps on my life jacket and drawn his shirt over himself and me, so I was under two shirts. It was the strangest feeling, floating there in the darkness. I'd get panicked every now and then, when I couldn't hear him breathing—we were only a few inches apart. Then he'd talk to me, calm me down. I got used to it after a while, I guess, because I was slipping in and out of sleep, a few hours later, when something brushed my leg and made me jump. Like I said, Daddy was standing up, probably sunk to his ankles in the muck. That still left a good five feet of water. I asked him if he had felt anything. He hadn't. But just as he said no, something hit us both at the same time, coming between us, I think. Daddy staggered back a step or two, slipping on the bottom.

A shark?

Probably. You always saw them there, a fin slicing through the water out in the channel. You looked for a second fin following the first, that's how you could tell it was a shark. Otherwise, it was just a dolphin with that horizontal fluke of a tail they've got. But that afternoon I'd seen the double fin easing through the water, maybe fifty feet out, sliding back and forth as easy as you please. It wasn't all that big a shark, maybe four foot or five, but big enough. I knew. So there I was, floating in the dark, remembering what I'd seen that afternoon and thinking about all the shark stories he'd ever told me. Not to mention that we weren't under the same shirt any more. I called out for him; I didn't know what had happened. I wanted him to hold me, so I started paddling forward, trying to find him. But then I heard his voice shouting to stay still. That's when I felt it again, its side scraping my khaki pants like sandpaper. I was crying, I remember, with Daddy half-whispering, hush, hush, they'll hear you. That really scared me. It hadn't occurred to me there might be more than one shark. 'And don't take a crap,' he warned, 'they love the smell of shit.'

So what happened?

Nothing. We didn't move for a minute or two—in the dark inside that shirt, all by myself, it felt like hours—and that was it. Gone. Daddy grabbed me and got us organized again. Only this time I stayed under his shirt, hanging on his neck till he said I was going to choke him. That's when he told me the story.

You were just ten years old?

Worse things happen to kids. It did make me sad, though, the story. I didn't know who I felt worse for, the captain or his little girl. But that's how we got through the night. That and the singing.

Singing?

After all those hours in the water, the life jacket wasn't working so well. Like everything else in the boat, the vests were army surplus, so God knows how much they'd been used already when we got them. I was floating lower and lower in the water; I had to tilt my head back after a while to keep it out of my mouth, the water. The cork had absorbed too much, I guess. I put my hands on my father's shoulders to keep from slipping deeper. Pretty soon, the life jacket was useless, but I kept it on for the sharks. At least, that was what I was thinking as I hung on to my father. He was having a hard time staying awake, so he started singing. It was the only song I ever heard him sing.

What was that?

I don't know its name, but it goes like this:

If the ocean were whiskey,
and I were a duck,
I'd swim to the bottom
and never come up.

But the ocean's not whiskey,
and I'm not a duck,
so I'll play the jack of diamonds
and trust to my luck.

He just kept singing those same verses over and over again, like a chant more than a song. Then I started singing. It must have sounded strange out there in that dark marsh, those two voices carrying across the water. We kept at it a long time, waiting for the light.

The whole night in the water?

The whole night. Then, when the sun rose, we hauled ourselves up into the boat. There were a few, straggling mosquitoes buzzing around us. I made a point of killing every one of them while Daddy tried the motor again. There was nothing doing, though, so Daddy tied a line to a bow cleat and, with water up to his chest, dragged the boat along the shelf of the mudflats for hours, it seemed, until he had hauled us to the mouth of the canal, where it joined the ship channel. He was so exhausted by the time we reached the edge of the flats he couldn't lift himself into the boat right away. He hung on by the gunnel, half-floating for a few minutes until he had the strength to swing his leg over the side. I pulled him into the boat, and he lay on the deck like a fish. Lying there, he heard the trill of a motor off in the distance. Then, out in the channel, we saw a shrimper, its butterfly nets up and drying in the sun after a night of trawling. We got up on the benches and swung the life vests over our heads, shouting in the still air. I've never known another feeling like the one when the shrimp boat, still a hundred, two hundred yards out, swung its bow towards us.

And they towed you in?

Yeah. Daddy offered the skipper twenty dollars for

his trouble and fuel. '*Oui, mon ami,*' he said—it was all still half-French and half-English back then—'but not for money.' So he towed us in to Pointe à la Hache. We tied the boat up, walked down a shell road, and found a little diner that was just opening. Daddy called home, told Mama to come get us. Then we started eating, and when she got there an hour and a half later, we were still eating.

My God, what a night.

Well, it wasn't over yet. We still had to drive back to Delacroix, where we'd launched, to get our other car and the trailer. Then, Mama and I drove home to New Orleans together while Daddy went back to Pointe à la Hache to get the boat. Every now and then she'd look at me and start crying. But it was funny. I wasn't hers anymore.

So that's how it happens? That's how they turn sweet little boys into big, mean men?

Something like that.

What was it he said? About the story, the story about the captain and his wife and daughter? You said that's what made you believe it.

When he got to the end of it, he said they had the photograph from the *Item*—the picture of those two columns of water, the one that ran in the paper—in some kind of archive on the third floor of the main library, down on Tulane Avenue.

Maybe that was part of the story he had heard?

No. What he said was all his own. He told me he had seen it once, the photograph, he and his father both. That's why I believed the story.

And that was all he said about it?

No, he said one other thing. Years later.

What was that?

He said they all end the same way, those sea stories. In madness or in death.

And what about this story?

It's not a story. It's true.

But how will it end?

End? With him singing, I guess, with the two of us singing—a man's deep, weary voice and a boy's thin little soprano, the voice of a drowned child, singing about whiskey and cards and a drunken duck—adrift in that black water, in that dark marsh, the mosquitoes hovering over our heads like death, and the two of us singing, singing until the sun comes up.

S.O.S.°

SEA
CREAT

URES

FROM *IN THE HEART OF THE SEA*
NATHANIEL PHILBRICK

The attack of the whaleship Essex *in 1820 by a sperm whale was only the beginning of a gruesome ordeal for its twenty-man crew. After the* Essex *sunk in the South Pacific, the crew set sail in three small boats for three months and covered 4,500 miles. The whale's fierce attack is said to be the inspiration for Herman Melville's* Moby-Dick.

Even today, in an age of instantaneous communication and high-speed transportation, the scale of the Pacific is difficult to grasp. Sailing due west from Panama, it is 11,000 miles to the Malay Peninsula—almost four times the distance Columbus sailed to the New World—and it is 9,600 miles from the Bering Strait to Antarctica. The Pacific is also deep. Hidden beneath its blue surface are some of the planet's most spectacular mountain ranges, with canyons that plunge more than six miles into the watery blackness.

Geologically, the volcano-rimmed Pacific is the most active part of the world. Islands rise up; islands disappear. Herman Melville called this sixty-four-million-square-mile ocean the "tide-beating heart of the earth."

By November 16, 1820, the *Essex* had sailed more than a thousand miles west of the Galapagos, following the equator as if it were an invisible lifeline leading the ship ever farther into the largest ocean in the world. Nantucket whalemen were familiar with at least part of the Pacific. Over the last three decades the coast of South America had become their own backyard. They also knew the western edge of the Pacific quite well. By the early part of the century, English whalers, most of them captained by Nantucketers, were regularly rounding the Cape of Good Hope and taking whales in the vicinity of Australia and New Zealand. In 1815, Hezekiah Coffin, the father of [George] Pollard's young cousin Owen, had died during a provisioning stop in the fever-plagued islands off Timor, between Java and New Guinea.

Lying between the island of Timor and the west coast of South America is the Central Pacific, what Owen Chase called "an almost untraversed ocean." The longitudes and latitudes of islands with names such as Ohevahoa, Marokinee, Owyhee, and Mowee might be listed in Captain Pollard's navigational guide, but beyond that they were— except for blood-chilling rumors of native butchery and cannibalism—a virtual blank.

All this was about to change. Unknown to Pollard, only a few weeks earlier, on September 29, the Nantucket whaleships *Equator* and *Balaena* stopped at the Hawaiian island of Oahu for the first time. In 1823, Richard Macy would be the first Nantucketer to provision his ship at the Society Islands, now known as French Polynesia. But as far as Pollard and his men knew in November of 1820, they were at the edge of an unknown world filled with unimaginable dangers. And if they were to avoid the fate of the ship they'd encountered at Atacames, whose men had almost died of scurvy before they could reach the South American coast for provisions, there was no time for far-flung exploration. It had taken them more than a month to venture out this far, and it would take at least that to return. They had, at most, only a few months of whaling left before they must think about returning to South America and eventually to Nantucket.

So far, the whales they had sighted in this remote expanse of ocean had proved frustratingly elusive. "Nothing occurred worthy of note during this passage," [Thomas] Nickerson remembered, "with the exception of occasionally chasing a wild shoal of whales to no purpose." Tensions mounted among the *Essex*'s officers. The situation prompted Owen Chase to make an adjustment aboard his whaleboat. When he and his boat-crew did finally approach a whale, on November 16, it was he, Chase reported, not his boat-steerer, Benjamin Lawrence, who held the harpoon.

This was a radical and, for Lawrence, humiliating turn of events. A mate took over the harpoon only after he had lost all confidence in his boatsteerer's ability to fasten to a whale. William Comstock told of two instances when mates became so disgusted with their boatsteerers' unsuccessful attempts to harpoon whales that they ordered them aft and took the iron themselves. One mate, Comstock wrote, screamed, "Who are you? What are you? Miserable trash, scum of Nantucket, a whimpering boy from the chimney corner. By Neptune I think you are afraid of a whale." When the boatsteerer finally burst into tears, the mate ripped the harpoon from his hands and ordered him to take the steering oar.

With Chase at the bow and Lawrence relegated to the steering oar, the first mate's boat approached a patch of water where, Chase predicted, a whale would surface. Chase was, in his own words, "standing in the fore part, with the harpoon in my hand, well braced, expecting every instant to catch sight of one of the shoal which we were in, that I might strike." Unfortunately, a whale surfaced directly under their boat, hurling Chase and his crew into the air. Just as had occurred after their first attempt at killing a whale, off the Falkland Islands, Chase and his men found themselves clinging to a wrecked whaleboat.

Given the shortage of spare boats aboard the *Essex*, caution on the part of the officers might have been expected, but caution, at least when it came to pursuing whales, was not part of the first mate's makeup. Taking to heart the old adage "A dead whale or a stove boat," Chase reveled in the risk and danger of whaling. "The profession is one of great ambition," he would boast in his narrative, "and full of honorable excitement: a tame man is never known amongst them."

Four days later, on November 20, more than 1,500 nautical miles west of the Galapagos and just 40 miles south of the equator, the lookout saw spouts. It was about eight in the morning of a bright clear day. Only a slight breeze was blowing. It was a perfect day for killing whales.

Once they had sailed to within a half mile of the shoal, the two shipkeepers headed the *Essex* into the wind with the maintopsail aback, and the three boats were lowered. The whales, unaware that they were being pursued, sounded.

Chase directed his men to row to a specific spot, where they waited "in anxious expectation," scanning the water for the dark shape of a surfacing sperm whale. Once again, Chase tells us, he was the one with the harpoon, and sure enough, a small whale emerged just ahead of them and spouted. The first mate readied to hurl the harpoon and, for the second time in as many days of whaling, ran into trouble.

Chase had ordered Lawrence, the ex-harpooner, to steer the boat in close to the whale. Lawrence did so, so close that as soon as the harpoon sliced into it, the panicked animal whacked the already battered craft with its tail, opening up a hole in the boat's side. As water poured in, Chase cut the harpoon line with a hatchet and ordered the men to stuff their coats and shirts into the jagged opening. While one man bailed, they rowed back to the ship. Then they pulled the boat up onto the *Essex*'s deck.

By this time, both Pollard's and Joy's crews had fastened to whales. Angered that he had once again been knocked out of the hunt, Chase began working on his damaged boat with a fury, hoping to get the craft operable while whales were still to be taken. Although he could have outfitted and lowered the extra boat (the one they had bargained for in the Cape Verde Islands, now lashed to the rack over the quarterdeck), Chase felt it would be faster to repair the damaged boat temporarily by stretching some canvas across the hole. As he nailed the edges of the canvas to the boat, his after oarsman, Thomas Nickerson—all of fifteen years old—took over the helm of the *Essex* and steered the ship toward Pollard and Joy, whose whales had dragged them several miles to leeward. It was then that Nickerson saw something off the port bow.

It was a whale—a huge sperm whale, the largest they'd seen so far—a male about eight-five feet long, they estimated, and approximately eighty tons. It was less than a hundred yards away, so close that they could see that its giant blunt head was etched with scars, and that it was pointed toward the ship. But this whale wasn't just large. It was acting strangely. Instead of fleeing in panic, it was floating quietly on the surface of the water, puffing occasionally through its blowhole, as if it were watching them. After spouting two or three times, the whale dove, then surfaced less than thirty-five yards from the ship.

Even with the whale just a stone's throw from the *Essex*, Chase did not see it as a threat. "His appearance and attitude gave us at first no alarm," he wrote. But suddenly the whale began to move. Its twenty-foot-wide tail pumped up and down. Slowly at first, with a slight side-to-side waggle, it picked up speed until the water crested around its massive barrel-shaped head. It was aimed at the *Essex*'s port side. In an instant, the whale was only a few yards away—"coming down for us," Chase remembered, "with great celerity."

In desperate hopes of avoiding a direct hit, Chase shouted to Nickerson, "Put the helm hard up!" Several other crew members cried out warnings. "Scarcely had the sound of the voices reached my ears," Nickerson remembered, "when it was followed by a tremendous crash." The whale rammed the ship just forward of the forechains.

The *Essex* shook as if she had struck a rock. Every man was knocked off his feet. Galapagos tortoises went skittering across the deck. "We looked at each other with perfect amazement," Chase recalled, "deprived almost of the power of speech."

As they pulled themselves up off the deck, Chase and his men had good reason to be amazed. Never before, in the entire history of the Nantucket whale fishery, had a whale been known to attack a ship. In 1807 the whaleship *Union* had accidentally plowed into a sperm whale at night and sunk, but something very different was happening here.

After the impact, the whale passed underneath the ship, bumping the bottom so hard that it knocked off the false keel—a formidable six-by-twelve-inch timber. The whale surfaced at the *Essex*'s starboard quarter. The creature appeared, Chase remembered, "stunned with the violence of the blow" and floated beside the ship, its tail only a few feet from the stern.

Instinctively, Chase grabbed a lance. All it would take was one perfectly aimed throw and the first mate might slay the whale that had dared to attack a ship. This giant creature would yield more oil than two, maybe even three, normal-sized whales. If Pollard and Joy also proved successful that day, they would be boiling down at least 150 barrels of oil in the next week—more than 10 percent of the *Essex*'s total capacity. They might be heading back to Nantucket in a matter of weeks instead of months.

Chase motioned to stab the bull—still lying hull-to-hull with the *Essex*. Then he hesitated. The whale's flukes, he noticed, were perilously close to the ship's rudder. If provoked, the whale might smash the delicate steering device with its tail. They were too far from land, Chase decided, to risk damaging the rudder.

For the first mate, it was a highly uncharacteristic display of caution. "But could [Chase] have foreseen all that so soon followed," Nickerson wrote, "he would probably have chosen the lesser evil and have saved the ship by killing the whale even at the expense of losing the rudder."

A sperm whale is uniquely equipped to survive a head-on collision with a ship. Stretching for a third of its length between the front of the whale's battering ram-shaped head and its vital organs is an oil-filled cavity perfectly adapted to cushioning the impact of a collision. In less than a minute, this eighty-ton bull was once again showing signs of life.

Shaking off its woozy lethargy, the whale veered off to leeward, swimming approximately six hundred yards away. There it began snapping its jaws and thrashing the water with its tail, "as if distracted," Chase wrote, "with rage and fury." The whale then swam to windward, crossing the *Essex*'s bow at a high rate of speed. Several hundred yards ahead of the ship, the whale stopped and turned in the

Essex's direction. Fearful that the ship might be taking on water, Chase had, by this point, ordered the men to rig the pumps. "[W]hile my attention was thus engaged," the first mate remembered, "I was aroused with the cry of a man at the hatchway, 'Here he is—he is making for us again.'" Chase turned and saw a vision of "fury and vengeance" that would haunt him in the long days ahead.

With its huge scarred head halfway out of the water and its tail beating the ocean into a white-water wake more than forty feet across, the whale approached the ship at twice its original speed—at least six knots. Chase, hoping "to cross the line of his approach before he could get up to us, and thus avoid what I knew, if he should strike us again, would prove our inevitable destruction," cried out to Nickerson, "Hard up!" But it was too late for a change of course. With a tremendous cracking and splintering of oak, the whale struck the ship just beneath the anchor secured at the cathead on the port bow. This time the men were prepared for the hit. Still, the force of the collision caused the whalemen's heads to jounce on their muscled necks as the ship lurched to a halt on the slablike forehead of the whale. The creature's tail continued to work up and down, pushing the 238-ton ship backward until—as had happened after the knockdown in the Gulf Stream—water surged up over the transom.

One of the men who had been belowdecks ran up onto the deck shouting, "The ship is filling with water!" A quick glance down the hatchway revealed that the water was already above the lower deck, where the oil and provisions were stored.

No longer going backward, the *Essex* was now going down. The whale, having humbled its strange adversary, disengaged itself from the shattered timbers of the copper-sheathed hull and swam off to leeward, never to be seen again.

o o o

The ship was sinking bow-first. The forecastle, where the black sailors slept, was the first of the living quarters to flood, the men's sea chests and mattresses floating on the rising tide. Next the water surged aft into the blubber room, then into steerage, where Nickerson and the other Nantucketers slept. Soon even the mates' and captain's cabins were awash.

As the belowdecks creaked and gurgled, the black steward, William Bond, on his own initiative, returned several times to the rapidly filling aft cabins to retrieve Pollard's and Chase's trunks and—with great foresight—the navigational equipment. Meanwhile Chase and the rest of the crew cut the lashing off the spare whaleboat and carried it to the waist of the ship.

The *Essex* began to list dangerously to port. Bond made one last plunge below. Chase and the others carried the whaleboat to the edge of the deck, now only a few inches above the ocean's surface. When the trunks and other equipment had been loaded aboard, everyone, including Bond, scrambled into the boat, the tottering masts and yards looming above them. They were no more than two boat lengths away when the *Essex*, with an appalling slosh and groan, capsized behind them.

Just at that moment, two miles to leeward, Obed Hendricks, Pollard's boatsteerer, casually glanced over his shoulder. He couldn't believe what he saw. From that distance it looked as if the *Essex* had been hit by a sudden squall, the sails flying in all directions as the ship fell onto her beam-ends.

"Look, look," he cried, "what ails the ship? She is upsetting!"

But when the men turned to look, there was nothing to see. "[A] general cry of horror and despair burst from the lips of every man," Chase wrote, "as their looks were directed for [the ship], in vain, over every part of the ocean." The *Essex* had vanished below the horizon.

The two boat-crews immediately released their whales and began rowing back toward the place the *Essex* should have been—all the time speculating frantically about what had happened to the ship. It never occurred to any of them that, in Nickerson's words, "a whale [had] done the work." Soon enough, they could see the ship's hull "floating upon her side and presenting the appearance of a rock."

As Pollard and Joy approached, the eight men crowded into Chase's boat continued to stare silently at the ship. "[E]very countenance was marked with the paleness of despair," Chase recalled. "Not a word was spoken for several minutes by any of us; all appeared to be bound in a spell of stupid consternation."

From the point at which the whale first attacked, to the escape from the capsizing ship, no more than ten minutes had elapsed. In only a portion of that time, spurred by panic, eight of the crew had launched an unrigged whale-boat from the rack above the quarterdeck, a process that would have normally taken at least ten minutes and required the effort of the entire ship's crew. Now, here they were, with only the clothes on their backs, huddled in the whaleboat. It was not yet ten in the morning.

It was then that Chase fully appreciated the service that William Bond had rendered them. He had salvaged two compasses, two copies of Nathaniel Bowditch's *New American Practical Navigator*, and two quadrants. Chase later called this equipment "the probable instruments of our salvation. . . . [W]ithout them," he added, "all would have been dark and hopeless."

For his part, Thomas Nickerson was swept by a sense of grief, not for himself, but for the ship. The giant black craft that he had come to know so intimately had been dealt a deathblow. "Here lay our beautiful ship, a floating and dismal wreck," Nickerson lamented, "which but a few minutes before appeared in all her glory, the pride and boast of her captain and officers, and almost idolized by her crew."

Soon the other two whaleboats came within hailing distance. But no one said a word. Pollard's boat was the first to reach them. The men stopped rowing about thirty feet away. Pollard stood at the steering oar, staring at the capsized hulk that had once been his formidable command, unable to speak. He dropped down onto the seat of his whaleboat, so overcome with astonishment, dread, and confusion that Chase "could scarcely recognize his countenance." Finally Pollard asked, "My God, Mr. Chase, what is the matter?"

Chase's reply: "We have been stove by a whale."

Even by the colossal standards of a sperm whale, an eighty-five-foot bull is huge. Today, male sperm whales, which are on average three to four times bulkier than females, never grow past sixty-five feet. Sperm whale expert Hal White-head has his doubts that the *Essex* whale could have been as large as Chase and Nickerson claimed it was. However, the logs of Nantucket whalemen are filled with references to bulls that, given the amount of oil they yielded, must have been on the order of the *Essex* whale. It is an established fact that whalemen in both the nineteenth and twentieth centuries killed male sperm whales in disproportionate numbers: not only were they longer than the females but the males' oil-rich spermaceti organs accounted for a larger portion of that length. In 1820, before a century and a half of selective killing had rid the world of large bulls, it may have indeed been possible to encounter an eighty-five-foot sperm whale. Perhaps the most convincing evidence resides in the hallowed halls of the Nantucket Whaling Museum. There, leaning against the wall, is an eighteen-foot jaw taken from a bull that was estimated to have been at least eighty feet long.

The sperm whale has the largest brain of any animal that has ever lived on earth, dwarfing even that of the mighty blue whale. The large size of the sperm whale's brain may be related to its highly sophisticated ability to generate and process sound. Just beneath its blowhole, a sperm whale has what the whalemen referred to as a monkey's muzzle, a cartilaginous clapper system that scientists believe to be the source of the clicking sounds it uses to "see" the world through echolocation. Whales also use clicking signals to communicate over distances of up to five miles. Females tend to employ a Morse code–like series of clicks, known as a coda, and male sperm whales make slower, louder clicks called clangs. It has been speculated that males use clangs to announce themselves to eligible females and to warn off competing males.

Whalemen often heard sperm whales through the hulls of their ships. The sound—steady clicks at roughly half-second intervals—bore such a startling similarity to the tapping of a hammer that the whalemen dubbed the sperm whale "the carpenter fish." On the morning of November 20, 1820, sperm whales were not the only creatures filling the ocean with clicking sounds; there was also Owen Chase, busily nailing a piece of canvas to the bottom of an upturned whaleboat. With every blow of his hammer against the side of the damaged boat, Chase was unwittingly transmitting sounds down through the wooden skin of the whaleship out into the ocean. Whether or not the bull perceived these sounds as coming from another whale, Chase's hammering appears to have attracted the creature's attention.

Chase maintained that when the whale first struck the ship, it was going about three knots, the velocity of a whale at normal cruising speed. Whitehead, whose research vessel was once bumped into by a pregnant whale, speculates that the bull might have even initially run into the *Essex* by mistake.

Whatever prompted the encounter, the whale was clearly not prepared for something as solid and heavy as a whaleship, which at 238 tons weighed approximately three times more than it did. The *Essex* might have been an old, work-worn whaleship, but she had been built to take her share of abuse. She was constructed almost entirely of white oak, one of the toughest and strongest of woods. Her ribs had been hewn from immense timbers, at least a foot square. Over that, laid fore and aft, were oak planks four inches square. On top of the planks was a sheathing of yellow pine, more than half an inch thick. Extending down from the waterline (the point of impact, according to Nickerson) was a layer of copper. The bull had slammed into a solid wooden wall.

What had begun as an experimental, perhaps unintentional jab with its head soon escalated into an all-out attack.

Like male elephants, bull sperm whales tend to be loners, moving from group to group of females and juveniles and challenging whatever males they meet along the way. The violence of these encounters is legendary. One whaleman described what happened when a bull sperm whale tried to move in on another bull's group:

> When the approaching bull attempted to join the herd, he was attacked by one of the established bulls, which rolled over on its back and attacked with its jaw. . . . Large pieces of blubber and flesh were taken out. Both bulls then withdrew and again charged at full tilt. They locked jaws and wrestled, each seemingly to try to break the other's jaw. Great pieces of flesh again were torn from the animals' heads. Next they either withdrew or broke their holds, and then charged each other again. The fight was even more

strenuous this time, and little could be seen because of the boiling spray. The charge and withdrawal were repeated two or three times before the water quieted, and then for a few seconds the two could be seen lying head to head. The smaller bull then swam slowly away and did not attempt to rejoin the cows. . . . A whaleboat was dispatched, and the larger bull was captured. The jaw had been broken and was hanging by the flesh. Many teeth were broken and there were extensive head wounds.

Instead of fighting with its jaws and tail—the way whales commonly dispatched whaleboats—the *Essex* whale rammed the ship with its head, something that, Chase insisted, "has never been heard of amongst the oldest and most experienced whalers." But what most impressed the first mate was the remarkably astute way in which the bull employed its God-given battering ram. Both times the whale had approached the vessel from a direction "calculated to do us the most injury, by being made ahead, and thereby combining the speed of the two objects for the shock." Yet, even though it had come at the *Essex* from ahead, the whale had avoided striking the ship directly head-on, where the ship's heavily reinforced stem, the vertical timber at the leading edge of the bow, might have delivered a mortal gash.

Chase estimated that the whale was traveling at six knots when it struck the *Essex* the second time and that the ship was traveling at three knots. To bring the *Essex* to a complete standstill, the whale, whose mass was roughly a third of the ship's, would have to be moving at more than three times the speed of the ship, at least nine knots. One naval architect's calculations project that if the *Essex* had been a new ship, her oak planking would have withstood even this tremendous blow. Since the whale did punch a hole in the bow, the *Essex*'s twenty-one-year-old planking must have been significantly weakened by rot or marine growth.

Chase was convinced that the *Essex* and her crew had been the victims of "decided, calculating mischief" on the part of the whale. For a Nantucketer, it was a shocking thought. If other sperm whales should start ramming ships, it would be only a matter of time before the island's whaling fleet was reduced to so much flotsam and jetsam.

Chase began to wonder what "unaccountable destiny or design" had been at work. It almost seemed as if something—could it have been God?—had possessed the beast for its own strange, unfathomable purpose. Whatever or whoever might be behind it, Chase was convinced that "anything but chance" had sunk the *Essex*.

After listening to the first mate's account of the sinking, Pollard attempted to take command of the dire situation. Their first priority, he announced, was to get as much food and water out of the wreck as possible. To do that, they needed to cut away the masts so that the still partially floating hull could right. The men climbed onto the ship and began to hack away at the spars and rigging with hatchets from the whaleboats. As noon approached, Captain Pollard shoved off in his boat to take an observation with his quadrant. They were at latitude 0°40' south, longitude 119°0' west, just about as far from land as it was possible to be anywhere on earth.

Forty-five minutes later, the masts had been reduced to twenty-foot stumps and the *Essex* was floating partly upright again, at a forty-five-degree angle. Although most of the provisions were unreachable in the lower hold, there were two large casks of bread between decks in the waist of the ship. And since the casks were on the *Essex*'s upper side, the men could hope that they were still dry.

Through the holes they chopped into the deck they were able to extract six hundred pounds of hardtack. Elsewhere they broke through the planks to find casks of freshwater—more, in fact than they could safely hold in their whaleboats. They also scavenged tools and equipment, including two pounds of boat nails, a musket, two pistols, and a small canister of powder. Several Galapagos tortoises swam to the whaleboats from the wreck, as did two skinny hogs. Then it began to blow.

In need of shelter from the mounting wind and waves, yet fearful the *Essex* might at any moment break up and sink like a stone, Pollard ordered that they tie up to the ship but leave at least a hundred yards of line between it and themselves. Like a string of ducklings trailing their mother, they spent the night in the lee of the ship.

The ship shuddered with each wave. Chase lay sleepless in his boat, staring at the wreck and reliving the catastrophe over and over again in his mind. Some of the men slept and others "wasted the night in unavailing murmurs," Chase wrote. Once, he admitted, he found himself breaking into tears.

Part of him was guilt-wracked, knowing that if he had only hurled the lance, it might have all turned out differently. (When it came time to write his own account of the attack, Chase would neglect to mention that he had the chance to lance the whale—an omission Nickerson made sure to correct in his narrative.) But the more Chase thought about it, the more he realized that no one could have expected a whale to attack a ship, and not just once but twice. Instead of acting as a whale was supposed to—as a creature "never before suspected of premeditated violence, and proverbial for its inoffensiveness"—this big bull had been possessed by what Chase finally took to be a very human concern for the other whales. "He came directly from the shoal which we had just before entered," the first mate wrote, "and in which we had struck three of his companions, as fired with revenge for their sufferings."

As they bobbed in the lee of the wreck, the men of the *Essex* were of no mind to debate the whale's motives. Their overwhelming question was how twenty men in three boats could get out of a plight like this alive.

DEATH IN THE MOONLIGHT
ARCHIBALD RUTLEDGE

If at night you happen to be standing up to your shoulders in salt water, when the wind is still and the tide is tranquil, in a creek not far from the ocean, and you suddenly feel a strange warm wave softly climb your neck and fondle your throat, all I have to say is, look out! I was so standing one moonlight night when just such a ghastly wave began to get intimate with me. Then terrible things happened, there in the murky water and the misty moonshine. A monster of the deep tried to do me to death—that's what happened. To this day I carry the physical scars of that encounter; and there's a scar on my mind too, a mute testimonial of my ordeal on that dread night.

My older brother and I had gone fishing down to the mouth of Ramshorn Creek. It was not sport with us, but a business. For several years we literally fished for a living. At night we used the gill-seine profitably in the mouths of creeks on the young floodtide. After setting the net entirely across the mouth of a creek, we would divide forces. I usually stayed by the seine and took out the mullets, whiting, school bass and other table fish as they gilled themselves. My brother took an oar and wandered up the edges of the creek, striking the water and otherwise disturbing the fish so that they would make a break down the estuary for the bay.

It was so on this night. I went into the water with no premonition of trouble. It was routine, and I had long been used to it. My raiment consisted merely of an old pair of trousers.

Deep night lay over the wide Carolina marshes, the mazy creeks that meandered lazily through them, the dim hummocks, the purple wall of the pinewood that marked the line of the mainland to westward. Far off could faintly be heard the soft roar of the surf falling sleepily on the drowsy shores of Cape Romain. Moonlight silvered the scene, touching with tender radiance the frayed reeds, the glimmering oyster-banks, the gleaming tide. But the light was not brilliant; a lacy mist lay here and there over the dim waters and the marsh.

I could hear all the night noises, with which I had long since been familiar: the rush of a school of fish in the shallow waters on the bay edge when a porpoise got after them; the melancholy grunting croak of a great blue heron; the mellow fluting of the willets; the weird intoning of a great horned owl from the dense red cedars on a lonely hummock. These sounds might make an amateur uneasy; but I was used to them all, and it was with our customary unconcern that my brother and I staked one end of our seine at the north side of Ramshorn Creek, and then, paying out the net as we rowed across the south, staked the other end at the south side. We had the long, winding estuary closed off. The boat we tied just outside the net so that I could conveniently throw the fish in as they were gilled.

There was a lot of phosphorescence in the water that night, and I could distinctly see the pale fiery outlines of some fish as they struck. But I did not enter the water until several energetic captives had begun to make it foam wildly near the surface. By this time my brother was two hundred yards up the creek, shouting and spanking the water with his oar to frighten the fish down.

When I thought that we had about a dozen mullets and sea-trout gilled, I waded into the warm water to begin taking them out. The water at its deepest part took me about the shoulders. I worked my way to the far side of the net and was almost halfway back across, with the water up to my breast, when suddenly it happened. At the time, I had my arms raised above my head, a big fish in each hand, just ready to heave them into the boat tied nearby.

Before this sinister stranger struck me, and just as I threw the poised fish, I was dimly aware of a monstrous show of phosphorescence and of a diabolical shape almost beside me. The next second the Thing massively brushed my left leg between the knee and the thigh, and instantly the salt water burned me like fire. When I ran my hand down in the water to see what had happened, I found that my trouser leg had been rasped away where this malignant phantom had bruised me, and that my leg was raw and bleeding.

At the same moment there came that ghoulish warm wave fondling my throat. In that creek mouth, there in the moonlight, with my brother far away, Death was upon me. I knew it. I felt it.

I was at close quarters with a white shark of huge proportions. He had drawn blood by rushing against me; his hide, as rough as sandpaper, had frayed both my clothing and my flesh. I looked wildly about and tried to discern in the water the position of this ruthless terror of the deep. I did not know which way to run. And all the while the placid moonlight slept on the world, and the willets fluted, and the faint echo of my brother's voice came to me from half a mile away.

As you can imagine, in my direful plight, all that I knew of the character and behavior of the white shark, a dread visitor from the West Indies into our waters, suddenly rushed over me. George Eagan had been killed by a shark in Bull's Bay. I had seen his body, and was sorry I had. In Wappoo Cut, Captain Fritz had been savagely mauled by one of these monsters, and had barely escaped with his life. By one of these prodigious brutes Charlie Deas had been killed in the surf at Sandy Point, within full sight of a dozen horrified bathers. And my own boyhood chum, Olaf Svensen, son of the keeper of Romain light, had met the same fate in Romain Inlet—not half a mile from where I now stood—literally in the jaws of death.

While every man is entitled to his opinion, I believe that a fifteen-foot white shark, on a blood trail at night, is about as fatal a creature as a man will ever encounter—especially since, in the water, a man is really out of his element. People need not talk to me about sharks being harmless. I have seen men dead by their killing. And I have had one of these burly ruffians after me.

In the midst of my wild thoughts, another wave washed me—this time going almost over my head. I plunged blindly for the shore, pulling on the seine to help me through the mud and water. While thus blundering madly toward the bank, and while I was thrusting my arms forward at full length to grip the seine to steady me and for a purchase to pull, I thrust my left hand up to the wrist full into the open mouth of the shark, now headed straight for me.

Whether he meant to seize me bodily or had his mouth partly open on account of his lust for the blood scent in the water, I do not know. But I know that I felt his cold hard lips and the serried ranks of his fearful teeth. I jerked my hand back and floundered madly for shore, his huge bulk knocking me heavily against the seine as I passed him. I was on the slope now, but the mud and water were deep, and at every instant I expected the barbarian to make his final rush and drag me down. What chance had I, or would any man have, against such an awful brute?

God knows why, but it never happened. I got out safely, and lay there on the bank in the mocking moonlight. My leg was stiff and sore, my side ached. When I looked down at my left hand, it was streaming blood. I found out after I got home that I had fourteen deep gashes in it— weird crisscross cuts and slashes from those razors in the monster's mouth. I tried to stand up and call my brother, but my voice failed me. I looked down at the sieve and suddenly saw both sustaining poles collapse violently into the water.

As the tide was flowing in, our commotion in the creek had not disturbed the waters of the bay, which shone tranquil and still. Through them now, as I gazed fascinated, I saw this murderous chimera, blazing in the lurid phosphorescence as if he were aflame, heading slowly seaward—an irresistible primal thing; cruel and cold, powerful, treacherous, ghoulish. Ghostly and pale in the haunting moonlight I saw his tall white dorsal fin cleave the water—like the periscope of some tremendous submarine about to deal death to its victim. I shivered as I watched that ponderous destroyer fade from sight. But for the mercy of God I might have been in those jaws, dead in the moonlit waters.

Whenever we went home, we hung up our net to dry. My brother did the work this night. The next morning I saw him standing by the seine, shaking his head as if to rid himself of an evil thought. As I came up he pointed to the net. Straight through the middle of it was a huge, ragged hole. When we measured it, we found it to be 2 feet 9 inches in diameter.

Although this incident happened thirty-five years ago, my scars as I have said, are still with me and with me still is the vivid memory of that dreadful placid night when Death stalked me in the moonlight.

DRUNKEN DIVING FOR POISON SEA SNAKES

TIM CAHILL

I recently traveled to the Philippines and chanced on a unique employment opportunity in the diving industry. The following is an outline of what you will need to know in order to get started in the glamorous and exciting field of drunken diving for poisonous sea snakes.

Where: From California, follow the Pacific Ocean west and south to the Philippine Sea. Make a sharp left turn and stop at the island of Cebu, in the Vasayan Sea. At the northern tip of the island is a jungle town called Daan Batayan, and a tad to the north is the village of Tapilon. Stand on the sandy shore and look west. That hummock standing dark against the setting sun is Gato Island. Gato is honeycombed by caves. Sea snakes spawn in the caves.

The Snakes: *Fasciata semifasciata* is an aquatic snake about four feet long and as big around as the business end of Dave Kingman's bat. The snake weighs over ten pounds and has alternating black and bluish-gray stripes. The skin is used to make purses and shoes. The meat and entrails are used as slop for hogs.

Fasciata semifasciata is definitely venomous. There is no argument on this point. In recent years, one diver died from a *Fasciata* bite. Generally, a bitten diver suffers only some swelling and numbness.

"My arm became the size of my leg and I couldn't move it for days because I couldn't feel it," is the way one diver described the result of a bite. The single recorded fatality may have been due to the victim's severe reaction to the venom. If you know you have an allergy to sea snake venom, perhaps drunken diving for poison sea snakes is not for you.

Equipment: The craftsmen of Daan Bantayan can make you a pair of goggles. These are carved from wood to conform to the contours of your face and they will fit no one else. Glass is glued to the wood and a headstrap is fashioned from an old automobile inner tube.

You'll need a flashlight and a clear plastic bag. The bag is placed over the flashlight and secured with tape, twine, tire-strips, and glue. This is your underwater light. Get an old tire and make two rubber bracelets, one for each wrist.

Preparing for Work: The snake divers believe that alcohol, taken internally in sufficient quantities, thins the blood and renders a bite less harmful. Any liquor will do, and the stronger the better. Rum, either Anejo or Manila, is good, but coconut wine flavored with anise, called malloroca, is favored by most of the divers. They particularly like Green Parrot brand. The wine is clear and thick and tastes like licorice. It comes in a clear beer-type bottle, the cork under the cap is usually black and a little crumbly.

The last resort is called tuba. This is the rapidly fermenting sap of the coconut palm, colored with mangrove bark. In the morning, the tuba gatherers bring in the daily crop. Fresh, the liquor is sweet, orange, and there's a white frost on the top. It is not very alcoholic and of little use to a snake diver. Tuba of a more aristocratic vintage—say three days—is more suited to your purpose. It's bitter as a lemon and will set you howling at the moon.

The Work: A few hours before sunset, you will head out across the bloodwarm Vasayan Sea in a dugout outrigger called a banca, powered by an eighteen-horsepower Briggs & Stratton engine. You'll relax in the bow and have some more rum—it takes an hour to cover the twelve miles to Gato.

The island is a little over an acre and perhaps two hundred feet high. Sheer rock walls rise about eighty feet, then give way to an inward-sloping tangle of dense brush. At water level, you will see many caves set deep into the rock walls. The water inside the caves is a deep blue— the same shade of blue you see inside of fastidious people's toilet bowls.

The snakes hide in little nooks and crannies during the day. You will do your diving at night, when they swarm inside the caves in their serpentine mating ballet.

Take one last sip of tuba, switch on your flashlight, slip into the dark water, and duck into the cave. Train your light on the water. Drop down about twenty feet to a ledge and hang there. On a lucky night, you'll be in the midst of a maelstrom of snakes. Grab one behind the head. The skin will be dry to the touch, not at all slimy.

To train yourself in the proper technique, grab your left thumb just below the knuckle with the thumb and first two fingers of your right hand. The snake is larger of course, but there is a knucklelike swelling just below the head where you want to grab him.

Now take the snake and slip his head under one of the rubber bracelets on your wrist. Find another snake. A good diver will surface with three snakes on either wrist.

What To Do If You Get Bit: Review Preparing for Work. Whether your medicine is rum, wine, or tuba, ingest an improbably excessive quantity. The boatmen will take you back in the banca. You will be lying on your back, drinking three-day tuba and singing some song half-remembered from your childhood. There will be a nasty paralytic numbness in your arm and it will swell like a goiter. You will probably not die. Snake divers seldom die. Keep repeating, "I will probably not die."

FROM *THE OLD MAN AND THE SEA*
ERNEST HEMINGWAY

It was on the third turn that he saw the fish first.

He saw him first as a dark shadow that took so long to pass under the boat that he could not believe its length.

"No," he said. "He can't be that big."

But he was that big and at the end of this circle he came to the surface only thirty yards away and the man saw his tail out of water. It was higher than a big scythe blade and a very pale lavender above the dark blue water. It raked back and as the fish swam just below the surface the old man could see his huge bulk and the purple stripes that banded him. His dorsal fin was down and his huge pectorals were spread wide.

On this circle the old man could see the fish's eye and the two gray sucking fish that swam around him. Sometimes they attached themselves to him. Sometimes they darted off. Sometimes they would swim easily in his shadow. They were each over three feet long and when they swam fast they lashed their whole bodies like eels.

The old man was sweating now but from something else besides the sun. On each calm placid turn the fish made he was gaining line and he was sure that in two turns more he would have a chance to get the harpoon in.

But I must get him close, close, close, he thought. I mustn't try for the head. I must get the heart.

"Be calm and strong, old man," he said.

On the next circle the fish's back was out but he was a little too far from the boat. On the next circle he was still too far away but he was higher out of water and the old man was sure that by gaining some more line he could have him alongside.

He had rigged his harpoon long before and its coil of light rope was in a round basket and the end was made fast to the bitt in the bow.

The fish was coming in on his circle now calm and beautiful looking and only his great tail moving. The old man pulled on him all that he could to bring him closer. For just a moment the fish turned a little on his side. Then straightened himself and began another circle.

"I moved him," the old man said. "I moved him then."

He felt faint again now but he held on the great fish all the strain that he could. I moved him, he thought. Maybe this time I can get him over. Pull, hands, he thought. Hold up, legs. Last for me, head. Last for me. You never went. This time I'll pull him over.

But when he put all of his effort on, starting it well out before the fish came alongside and pulling with all his strength, the fish pulled part way over and then righted himself and swam away.

"Fish," the old man said. "Fish, you are going to have to die anyway. Do you have to kill me too?"

That way nothing is accomplished, he thought. His mouth was too dry to speak but he could not reach for the water now. I must get him alongside this time, he thought. I am not good for many more turns. Yes you are, he told himself. You're good for ever.

On the next turn, he nearly had him. But again the fish righted himself and swam slowly away.

You are killing me, fish, the old man thought. But you have a right to. Never have I seen a greater, or more beautiful, or a calmer or more noble thing than you, brother. Come on and kill me. I do not care who kills who.

Now you are getting confused in the head, he thought. You must keep your head clear. Keep your head clear and know how to suffer like a man. Or a fish, he thought.

"Clear up, head," he said in a voice he could hardly hear. "Clear up."

Twice more it was the same on the turns.

I do not know, the old man thought. He had been on the point of feeling himself go each time. I do not know. But I will try it once more.

He tried it once more and he felt himself going when he turned the fish. The fish righted himself and swam off again slowly with the great tail weaving in the air.

I'll try it again, the old man promised, although his hands were mushy now and he could only see well in flashes.

He tried it again and it was the same. So he thought, and he felt himself going before he started; I will try it once again.

He took all his pain and what was left of his strength and his long gone pride and he put it against the fish's agony and the fish came over onto his side and swam gently on his side, his bill almost touching the planking of the skiff and started to pass the boat, long, deep, wide, silver and barred with purple and interminable in the water.

The old man dropped the line and put his foot on it and lifted the harpoon as high as he could and drove it down with all his strength, and more strength he had just summoned, into the fish's side just behind the great chest fin that rose high in the air to the altitude of the man's chest. He felt the iron go in and he leaned on it and drove it further and then pushed all his weight after it.

Then the fish came alive, with his death in him, and rose high out of the water showing all his great length and width and all his power and his beauty. He seemed to hang in the air above the old man in the skiff. Then he fell into the water with a crash that sent spray over the old man and over all of the skiff.

The old man felt faint sick and he could not see well. But he cleared the harpoon line and let it run slowly through his raw hands and, when he could see, he saw the fish was on his back with his silver belly up. The shaft of the harpoon was projecting at an angle from the fish's shoulder and the sea was discolouring with the red of the blood from his heart. First it was dark as a shoal in the blue water that was more than a mile deep. Then it spread like a cloud. The fish was silvery and still and floated with the waves.

The old man looked carefully in the glimpse of vision that he had. Then he took two turns of the harpoon line around the bitt in the bow and laid his head on his hands.

"Keep my head clear," he said against the wood of the bow. "I am a tired old man. But I have killed the fish which is my brother and now I must do the slave work."

THE MERMAID
JULIA BLACKBURN

The man was still there poised in indecision and staring
at the thing which lay heaped at his feet. I saw then that it
was not a human corpse, or the trunk of a tree, or a bundle
of sail that he had found, but a mermaid. She was lying face
down, her body twisted into a loose curl, her hair matted
with scraps of seaweed.

The year was fourteen hundred and ten and it was
very early in the morning with the sun pushing its way
gently through a covering of mist that floated aimlessly
over the land and the water.

The man had never seen a mermaid before except
for the one carved in stone above the east door of the
church. She had very pointed teeth and a double tail like
two soft and tapering legs, while this one had a single tail
which could have belonged to a large halibut or a cod.

The man stepped forward and squatted down
beside her. The pattern of her interlinking scales glinted

with an oily light. He stroked them along the direction in which they lay and they were wet and slippery leaving a coating of slime on his palm. But when his hand moved over the pale skin of her back it was as rough as a cat's tongue and very dry and cold.

He lifted a hank of dark hair, feeling its weight. Little transparent shrimps were tangled within its mesh and struggling to free themselves. A yellow crab scuttled around the curve of the waist and dropped out of sight.

He hesitated for a moment but then he took hold of the mermaid's shoulders and rolled her over. The sand clung in patches on her body like the map of some forgotten country. Her nipples were as red as sea anemones. Her navel was deep and round. Her eyes were wide open and as blue as the sky could ever be. As he gazed at her a lopsided smile drifted over her face.

He had presumed that she was dead and with the shock of her being alive he let out a cry and jumped to his feet. He turned and began to run as fast as he could over the ridges of muddy sand and towards the village.

I watched as he trampled on the grey scrub of sea lavender and the low samphire bushes, their thin skins so easily broken. But he trod more carefully once he had reached the strip of pale stones littered with the sharp empty shells of clams and oysters, until with his heart thumping in his throat he was beside the fishing boats and the wooden hut battered out of shape by the north wind.

The old fisherman was sitting there just as before, singing to himself as he mended his nets with his legs stretched out stiffly in front of him and his bones aching.

He made no response as the young man tried to explain what the sea had thrown on to the land; he didn't even raise his head to look at the speaker.

The young man ran on again until he had arrived at the first house of the village. The shoemaker's wife was standing by the door, her arms cradling a huge belly which seemed to be about to split open like a ripe fruit.

'There is a mermaid!' he said to her, but she was lost in thought and hardly heard him although her baby lurched violently inside her womb as if it was shocked by the news. She remembered that later.

The man went into the house and from a back room he fetched one of those narrow wooden spades that are used for digging lugworms. Then he returned the way he had come. He meant to bury the mermaid even if she was still alive and his task made him walk slowly now, with all the solemnity of an executioner.

He looked out across the expanse of sand shimmering like an ocean of calm water. He saw how a flock of gulls had settled in a noisy mass on the place where the mermaid was lying and as he drew closer they lifted, screaming and turning into the air.

But the mermaid had gone. Nothing remained of her except for a single lock of dark hair which resembled a ribbon of torn seaweed.

Nevertheless the man dug a hole as deep as a grave: the salty water seeping into it, the sides crumbling away and seeming to melt like snow. And as he dug the surface brightness of the sand was replaced by greasy layers of black and grey mud smelling of age and decay.

When the hole was ready he picked up the hair and dropped it in, covering it over quickly and stamping it down. He marked the place with a big black stone.

That evening he sat with the old fisherman drinking from a jug of beer and going over and over the story of what he had seen and what he had done. During the night his wife Sally shook him awake because she could hear the sound of a woman crying, desperate and inconsolable. On the following morning a cow died for no good reason and the shoemaker's wife gave birth to a baby with the head of a monstrous fish which only lived for a few hours.

Everyone agreed that this must be the mermaid's fault and they told the priest to do something. So the priest went with the man to where the hair was buried. He took a holy candle with him but it kept on going out in the wind, and he had a bottle of holy water to sprinkle over the sand. In his spidery handwriting he had copied three paternosters on to a piece of parchment and he tucked this under the black stone while reciting a prayer to protect them all from harm.

After that things were quiet again for a while but it was as if a lid had been clamped down on a pot that was bound to boil over sooner or later. The mermaid had disturbed the pattern of life in the village. People waited with growing apprehension for what might follow.

The priest had a dream in which she slithered over his body like a huge eel and wrapped her tail tight around his legs. He was crying when he woke up.

The man who had stroked her rough skin kept on stumbling against her image in a corner of his mind.

Whenever he went out with his boat he would hope to find her glistening among the fish he had caught in his nets. Searching for her, he began to travel further and further from the shore.

s.o.s.

UNDER

THE WAVES

DIVING BEYOND LIMITS
NEIL SIMON

On a recent dive trip to the Turks and Caicos Islands, I had the opportunity to go deep diving with an experienced crew of divers. We chose the island of Provo, known for water temperatures in the low 80s and visibility reaching 200 feet, and planned to descend 255 feet down a coral reef wall that just been discovered by a local skipper. I was giddy with an excitement laced with fear from the moment I learned of the opportunity, through the dive plan on the plane, right up to the moment the tip of my fins broke the mercury-like surface of the Caribbean Sea a week later.

I had been diving for several years and always dreamed about the day I would defy the voice of reason and embark on a dive beyond the limits of what I had been taught as a dive student. The recreational diving recommended limit is 130 feet. The probability of experiencing a fatal complication, physical or mental, increases exponentially the deeper one goes. Deep diving is a controversial activity. Some believe that regardless of experience, it is very dangerous. Others maintain that with technical proficiency, deep diving is no more dangerous than diving within the recreational limit. I can still hear the words of my first instructor as she described the area on the dive tables of both physiological and psychological danger. "Dive in the black, you don't come back," she used to say. (Ironically, I later found out that she was herself a confessed, addicted deep diver—something she chose to leave off her diving résumé.)

I had worked on the Bering Sea as a commercial longline fisherman and been a surfer all my life. So I felt close to the sea and, perhaps foolishly, a little immune to its dangers. But my work experience in Alaska had instilled in me a respect to nearly religious proportions for the sea's power, and I was not going to pass up the deep-diving experience, no matter what the risk.

As we raced to the dive spot across the ocean's unusually calm surface, I felt nervous as my brother Alain and I made last moment gear checks to one another's kit. It was like rock climbing, I reasoned. You're not really a lead climber until you take that first horrendous fall.

There was little room for talking over the roar of the twin V6 outboards humming along at full throttle by the dive platform. My focus on that boat ride was intense, very much as if the dive was a matter of life or death, which in a way, all deep dives are. One thing was for certain, the skipper, a salty pirate named Fi Fi, who served in COFUSCO, the French equivalent of the Navy Seals, wasn't wasting any time to get us to his latest discovery.

Upon entering the water in one giant stride off the back of the boat, I felt calm. All the anticipation and anxiety I had been feeling seemed to dissipate immediately once the water covered my skin. I quickly took one breath off my regulator and began to descend. With only one tank of air per person and an intended bottom time of roughly five minutes, we wasted little time in getting started on the long kick down. Following the lead of my brother, an experienced deep diver for more than 20 years, I felt confident and well prepared. We had discussed in our pre-dive preparation a simple system of hand multiplications that would enable us to check on each other's awareness as we went deeper.

As we vigorously kicked past the flat sands meeting the lip of the wall at 60 feet, where conches graze and grass eels abound, I reminded myself not to panic, no matter what was to happen. I concentrated on breathing slowly and remained focused. We went headfirst over the wall.

Our fins moved us rapidly down the façade of the coral and sponge. Upside down, I watched the kaleidoscope of colors rush before my eyes. This was truly an epic dive spot. A huge red elephant ear sponge the size of a Volkswagen Bug greeted us as we forged past the lip. Alain looked at me with eyes bulging in surprise at its size. I could feel the tingling sensation of tiny air bubbles brush upon my body hairs as they raced towards the surface. The visibility was an amazing 200-plus feet. Before I knew it, we were at 140 feet and still kicking.

Continuing deeper, the light began to dim and the sponges lessened in size and intensity of color. A pale gray hue engulfed all color except blue. As you dive deeper, light dissipates and, beginning with red, the colors of the spectrum gradually disappear. There were no longer myriads of rainbow-colored fish. We stopped at 180 feet and looked around. My breathing had slowed to an unnaturally relaxed pace, similar to breathing during deep sleep. I could hear the low throb of my heart echo throughout the veins in my body. Faint traces of metallic silver sounds reverberated in my mind as I exhaled.

I slowly read my air pressure gauge as my brother monitored our dive plan on his Beauchat computer: 1900 psi (pounds per square inch of pressure). Very good, I thought to myself. My brother signaled a double okay signal and I signaled back. He turned his thumb downward, and I gave a brief nod of approval, after which he told me with his hands to multiply three times two times two. I breathed, computed, breathed, computed some more and answered. I got it right, and he smiled big at me. We could go deeper.

As we gradually descended past the 200-foot mark, I looked up very slowly and saw the sun shimmering on the surface of the water. I couldn't be feeling its warmth at this depth, yet I felt like I was. The wall was to my right, and to my left was a void that can only be compared to that of the sky at night—except it was a deep psychedelic blue and had no stars.

When I first looked left, I felt my heart stutter in my chest and knew instantly that its beating was reflexive and yet voluntary, somehow linked to my will. This scared me because I felt my heart could stop at any moment if I wanted it to. That was how slow it was beating. When I began to hear a chorus of sounds with every exhalation of breath, I realized that I had become *narced*—an expression used by divers to describe a nitrogen-induced high. The feeling at that depth, given my body weight and body-fat percentage, was the rough equivalent of drinking four martinis in as many minutes. But it was in no way the dull high you might experience from alcohol at the surface, this was something else. Something spiritual.

The pauses of silence between my breaths had become longer than the actual moments of breathing themselves. I cannot recall a time in my life in which I felt so close to death, as if the sea could so easily consume and silence the breath in my lungs. It was an incredibly humbling but peaceful feeling.

One more time I was given the okay signal, and one more time I signaled back that I was all right. However, I didn't feel that I knew who exactly was doing the signaling and who I was signaling to. Things were no longer working right in my mind, but because it still felt like a strange and yet comfortably clear haze, I proceeded. As I watched the fingers on Alain's hand ask me to multiply eight times four, I became utterly perplexed. So, with no answer, he signaled once more. I jump-kicked whatever it is that gives answers to things like this and thought 32.

At first I could not make my fingers signal back. It was as though they were suddenly entities separate from myself and needed to be tended like the strings of a puppet. Upon making them work and giving the correct answer, Alain signaled okay once more and gave me the thumbs-down motion. My brain felt like it was in mud, and yet it felt so damn good—like all intelligence is artificial anyway at 200-plus feet of water. So I continued on cautiously, following instinct through a serene fog of quasi-euphoric thoughtlessness.

We gradually descended to our final depth of 225 feet, at which point I can honestly say that there was nobody home in my head. There was a very slow, very deep breathing process going on and that was it. My eyes looked around in complete awe as we both scanned the underwater horizon only to be greeted by a ten-foot reef shark cruising the periphery of our vision. My brother pointed to it as a I nodded back. I felt like I was three years old, drinking chocolate milk and watching my favorite cartoon. I knew that shark personally; I was his best friend. I was him undulating through the warm blue water at the edge of the void.

Once again I looked up and saw what felt like 10,000 feet of water separating us from the warm breezes that blew at the surface. I could feel the sun as it entered the spot between the two eyebrows on my forehead. The ocean wall had many layers like the contours of the great mountain, something I hadn't noticed on our descent. It was carved by the hand of some power so great I felt it an equally powerful honor just to be able to witness its magnificent shapes. About 120 feet above us, some other divers in our party swam like tiny slow-moving insects.

Hearing the beep of the dive computer was like being awakened from a great dream by your alarm clock on a Monday morning. My trance was broken and replaced by the knowledge that our stay was over. Now we had to make our way cautiously back to the surface to decompress. We moved at a rate no greater than one foot per second to avoid decompression sickness, an umbrella term for all the problems that can occur at such depth (like the bends or an air embolism, where air bubbles burst through the air sacs of the lung wall).

Our stay at 225 feet was brief, but the dive would forever cement our reverence for the sea, like a tattoo you might get in an intoxicated stupor. Only this drunkenness was not alcohol induced; it was an intoxication with the awesome beauty of the sea. The nitrogen in my blood helped create this vision, but nitrogen was not its cause. The nitrogen affected my experience in the same way peyote might help a Native American shaman access an altered state of mind.

We took momentary breaks in our ascent, at about 120, 80 and 60 feet. Finally, at 15 feet, spare air tanks tethered onto a safety stop bar under the boat left us hanging like a couple of fetuses sucking air through long rubber hoses in total ecstasy. How right I was in embarking on this dive; the reward truly outweighed the risk.

In all my years alive on this planet as Neil Simon, I knew the sacred bliss of deep diving before I actually made my triumphant first deep dive. Some will say that deep diving is nothing more than a nitrogen-induced high, but others like myself can tell a whole different story, one that brings me back quickly and peacefully to the sacred force of creation that was my lonely heartbeat as I stared at the sun from deep within the womb of the sea.

RHAPSODY IN BLUE

JESSICA MAXWELL

Jonah.

I was thinking about Jonah. In fact I couldn't stop thinking about Jonah, which, if you are one of several hundred human anchovies packed into the belly of a 747 jet vamoosolating through space somewhere above the Pacific Ocean, is not exactly a pleasant obsession. I tried to tune my headset to the Muzak channel so some horrible song like "Feeeeelings" would get stuck in my brain instead, but all I could get was Hawaiian music. Which made things worse. We were en route to Honolulu which my mind translated as "en route to Honolulu" because it was still stuck on Jonah and insisting on picturing us baked into this whale of a metal pastry like a bunch of little tourist McNuggets who only *thought* they were heading for a good tan. Fine. Maybe ninety-nine percent of us were. But *this* muchacha was looking down the throat of a blind date with Muhammad Ali of the Deep Blue Sea. I was going swimming with whales the next day and this Jonah thing was getting on my nerves.

Okay, I wasn't *really* going swimming with whales, unless I had about $25,000 in loose change, which is the Hawaiian Department of Fisheries' fine for intentionally paddling around in whale territory without a permit in the merry month of February. That's when about 2,000 hump-back whales show up off the island of Maui for their annual winter vacation. Like everyone else coming to Hawaii this time of year, the whales are only interested in hanging out in the sun and making a lot of whoopie, which is why it's a federal offense to bug them. This is their breeding season, their calving season too, and they've got enough problems with all the boat and plane and jet ski traffic around Maui without some ridiculous dwarfette water-nerd with terrible eyesight and silly black chicken feet snorkeling around in their bedroom.

However. Reliable fishy sources had informed me that should one get in the water *any*where off Maui one has a pretty good chance of hearing humpbacks *singing*. Their songs are so loud and carry so far that you could probably hear whale song from your hotel bathtub if you paid atten-tion. It is, in fact, common to hear humpback solos from the shore.

"That ought to give all these sunstroke candidates a thrill," I thought meanly, regarding the stockyard full of tender white meat seated around me pretending to be engrossed in the dumb Demi Moore movie playing on the miniature screen about a whale's length down the aisle. From that distance Demi and her various love interests looked about as interesting as sand fleas—in fact they looked a lot *like* sand fleas—so I snubbed the movie and continued to search for a suitably sappy musical substitute for my Jonah Jones (it is a scientific fact that the cerebral stickiness of melodies is directly proportionate to their dork quotient, which explains why ninety-five percent of all Americans spend the better part of December humming "fa-la-la-la-la-la-la-la-la"). But my channel-hopping accidentally cut into the movie dialogue wherein Demi was telling the fortune of a severely buttoned-down woman who looked like the only future she could possible use was a couple of bottles of Cuervo Gold and a night on the town with Bruce Willis.

"Ah . . . ah see ya'll singin'," Demi drawled.

"I do sing in the church choir," the woman replied prissily.

"No," Demi insisted. "I see ya'll in a nightclub."

"A psychic," I thought, not liking at all what I was thinking. "Demi Moore is a psychic talking about singing, Jonah was a prophet *and* the only person in history to be eaten by a whale AND I'M GOING SWIMMING WITH SINGING WHALES IN THE MORNING!"

"Well, it wasn't a humpback whale," Kona Joe was saying as he slowly maneuvered our boat out of Lahaina Harbor which had recently been made a humpback sanctuary. "It had to have been a sperm whale—that's the only species whose esophagus is wide enough to swallow a man. It *would* be creepy though," he agreed. "Sliding around in there with a bunch of thirty-foot squid. Yick!"

Then glanced at my face, which probably looked a lot like Demi Moore's when she realized that the short, fat butcher she had just married was *not* the cosmically intended love-of-her-life.

"Look," Kona Joe offered sweetly, "you have a *much* greater chance of being eaten by a shark than a whale."

"Is she *still* whining?" Art Wolfe inquired sympathetically, having graciously stowed his several dozen camera bags all over the back of the boat, making falling overboard a distinct possibility. He is, of course, America's most famous *and* fearless wildlife photographer, having cut his Fujichrome teeth on wolves, bears and bellowing Alaska moose. Unfortunately, he was right. I *was* whining. I was, in fact, being a weenie. Art, as usual, was being Hans Franz.

"I'm Hans Franz and ve're going hafter vhales or I plant you six feet under!" he hollered to Kona Joe who hollered back: "Listen to me yesterday, don't remember me tomorrow!"

And we were off.

Kona Joe's Boston Whaler *Outrage* ripped along the watery corridor between Maui and Lanai, the pineapple island. The sea looked bluer than your usual maritime blue, sort of a Technicolor hybrid of Prussian blue and lapis, not turquoise but not navy either. The Christmas geometry of Maui revolved by on our left, yokes of emerald sugar cane fields girded with the island's blood-colored earth. Clouds snagged themselves on the West Maui Mountains throwing milky light all over this tropical farmland. It was hard to believe the ecological disaster sugar cane had brought to the place. The soil was trashed and the toxic run-off of pesticides alone had finally caused a weird species of algae to invade Maui's beaches.

"Whale spout, dead starboard, mates!" Art yelled in a disgraceful pirate impersonation.

There were, in fact, two. Then three. Possibly four. Whale spouts, that is, not pirates.

"Might be a heat rush," Kona Joe announced and nosed the boat in the whales' general direction. He meant that we might have happened upon several males vying for the favors of one female. It was clear that Kona Joe knew his humpback sociology.

He ought to. A native of the Big Island, Kona Joe is himself some kind of legendary itinerant underwater photographer who specializes in reef fish—God only knows where Art found him. These wildlife guys have this mystical international photographers' network whose members always know when someone important is shooting in their territory and they often show up to help out. Kona Joe had volunteered to take Art within the legal viewing range of Maui's humpbacks, which means no closer than 100 yards.

"Nah, it's just a warm rush," Kona Joe diagnosed once we'd caught up with the whales.

"What's the difference?" I asked.

"It's just mild mating fever with a little aggressive behavior—some fin slapping, a little bubble blowing, no Academy Award performances."

"You oughta be in pictures!" Art sang as his camera clicked away. Four good-sized humpbacks sort of loitered along off the boat's bow, roiling around, occasionally ramming into each other, and often fwopping each other on the head with twelve-foot pectoral fins like an ocean-going Four Stooges routine.

"That's a good-sized pod," Kona Joe said.

"I've been thinking podsitively all morning," Art replied.

Suddenly huge, blooping bubbles surfaced off the right side of the boat.

"Hang on!" Kona Joe cried. "One's going under us!"

I had already been through this in Southeast Alaska. Art and I had flown up to Glacier Bay last August to witness the northern end of the Pacific humpbacks' migration, which amounts to your basic whale feeding frenzy. Once they leave Alaska in the fall, humpbacks don't eat again until they return the following spring. We had watched in awe as they chased their breakfast around and under our boat, swimming open-mouthed while their multiple plates of baleen filtered out gallons of fresh Alaskan krill.

But here in Paradise the main social activity is beating the hell out of each other, among the male whales anyway. Battles over females are fierce and bloody. You don't want to get in their way.

Maui researchers have found only one thing that genuinely distracts humpbacks from their erotic business at hand: food songs. "It's common knowledge around here that somebody recorded the sounds whales make while feeding in Alaska," Kona Joe informed us. "Then they played it underwater here in Maui."

"What happened?" I asked.

"They got absolutely rushed by whales."

"Then what happened?"

"Well, the whales swam around them a while, then when they figured out it was a hoax, they left."

"Those scientists are lucky the whales didn't turn them into hors d'oeuvres themselves," Art spat.

"Look! A blue fin!" I yelled as a narrow, wing-shaped, turquoise pectoral suddenly slid by the boat.

"It's white," Kona Joe corrected. "The water makes it look blue."

These humpbacks were getting a little too close for comfort, just like they did in Alaska. *My* comfort, anyway. Art, of course, was happily burning film. He was getting some great, leviathanian leaps framed by the high-toned drama of Maui's Olowalu Valley rising visionlike in the background.

But I was there to hear whales sing, and if more than one male humpback is around, *nobody* sings. Researchers have proven that singers are almost exclusively male and almost all singing is done during mating season. And we're not talking little two-minute Top Forties riffs, either. Humpback whale song is a serious, complex and personalized art, the sonatas of the animal kingdom. The songs themselves are carefully remembered and deeply patterned musical compositions which, when played at fast-forward, are identical to bird song. And when they're played backward they sound like Harry Connick, Jr., on helium . . . oh, I'm *just* kidding.

Humpback songs have driven sailors—not to mention female whales—Looney Tunes for thousands of years. You can imagine sailing into Bermuda after about three months at sea and hearing loud, moaning trumpet-shrieks blamming through the hull of your ship in the middle of the night. I guess you *would* be intrigued. It was, in fact, the U.S. Navy that first recorded humpback songs back in the 1950s. And the first to recognize their intricate, repetitive detailing were whale researchers Katherine and Roger Payne.

"Within each population, all humpbacks share the same song," writes Katherine Payne in the March 1991 issue of *Natural History*. "[It's] a long sequence of varied sounds organized in patterns that...can be described as having phrases (groups of notes that are roughly the same each time they are repeated) and themes (groups of similar phrases)."

And it was biologists Katherine Payne and Linda Guinee who made the remarkable discovery that humpbacks actually use rhyme to remember their longest songs: "Analysis of the songs shows that when they contain many themes, they also include rhymelike material, phrases with similar sounding endings. . . . When songs contain few themes, we do not hear this sort of material."

She notes that each song is "constantly evolving" and that "individual whales always keep up with the current version of their population's song."

Thus, the song sung at the beginning of the humpback breeding season is not the same song sung at the end of it. Since whales stay pretty quiet when they're not breeding, one would expect these Hawaiian crooners to utterly forget last year's song during their six-month Alaskan feast. But, when they cruise back into Maui the following year, they all sing *exactly the same song they were singing at the end of last year's breeding season.*

"Singing, not silence, is what brings on change," Katherine Payne explains, "and the song changes most and fastest when the most whales are singing."

Like the living human language, humpback songs, then, are cultural invention, not Neanderthal blithering repeated over and over ad whale nauseam across the millennium. So the song you hear at any given moment will remain the same for about a week, then it's gone forever, kind of like pop music of the deep blue sea.

It was noon and the ocean had been relatively quiet.

"I think we've hit a whale-free zone," Kona Joe observed. "But keep looking—even a strange wave can look like a whale."

At that moment, like a giant, visual, double entendre, *two* humpbacks breached clean out of the water not half a mile off the bow of our boat.

"A double breach!" Art breathed. "I've *never* seen that."

"Me either," Kona Joe said. "Whoa."

Within minutes the whales breached again, one visibly smaller than the other. Either this was a humpback version of Driver's Ed. or one amorous couple was practicing for the Whale Winter Olympics. Art took his station behind his tripod which he'd set up on the boat's bow, then watched helplessly as the tandem jumpers breached a third time, this time even farther away.

"What a couple of blubberheads," Kona Joe sighed. "They jump all day, they jump all night. They almost never get it right."

"Sounds like a song," Art replied.

"A whale mating song," I added. "Speaking of songs, can we take a break from the camera thing and look for a singer?"

"Whats-a-matter, you got lens envy?" Art enquired tactfully.

An annoyed-looking flying fish launched itself out of the water and almost hit him in the teeth. Nonetheless, the Whale Gods denied my request. For the rest of the day we saw a goodly amount of whale spouts, fin flapping, tail wagging and heart-stopping breaches that finally drove Kona Joe to unsheathe his own camera and join Art on the prow of the boat. But we did not hear a single singer. Finally, Kona Joe announced that it was Snorkel Time.

"Gentlemen," he said, "lower your lenses."

"You *cannot* laugh *and* snorkel at the same time," Kona Joe called down from the boat. It was too late. The butterfly fish had tickled my face again and I was about to choke to death.

Kona Joe had motored us over to some of his favorite snorkeling water off a quiet side of the island of Lanai. Art and I had struggled into our wet suits and flippers, then dork-walked over to the boat's ladder and flapped on into the sea. I fully intended to hang onto the bottom of the ladder while I cased the place for sharks, and to my surprise, Art did too.

"I'm not a real strong swimmer," he confided, which through his snorkel sounded more like some kind of Arabic prayer. But Art had sunk a ton of money into his new underwater camera and a pair of twin headlight-like water-proof flashes. He needed tropical fish photos for a future book, and damn if he wasn't going to get them. So he bravely ventured a few feet away from the boat while I clung to it like a baby sea horse afraid to swim on my own. Finally, I forced myself to look under the water.

What I saw was glorious. A wide, brightly lit world filled with transparent turquoise water and finished with a compelling assortment of colorful ocean floor sea things, many of which looked like brains-on-drugs. I was sure those were giant clams and, being the world's worst distance estimator, privately wondered if it were possible for one to bite the tip of my flipper until I actually *looked* at my flippers and realized that they were probably a good thirty feet away from the nearest clam mouth.

That established, I released one hand and, keeping the other firmly attached to the ladder, I paddled around in, oh, I'd say, about a four centimeter diameter. At which point Kona Joe sneakily forced my other hand off the ladder by smushing crunched-up tortilla chips into it. And, Whapp-o, I was instantly attacked by several million electric yellow fishes that *came out of nowhere*. And, naturally, if *they* could be hiding right in front of your face, so could Jaws.

But I didn't have much time to consider that comforting thought because several kazillion little black fish—durgons—had suddenly shown up too, fighting viciously with the yellow fish—millet seed butterfly fish—for the stupid corn chips which were still stuffed into my fist. In desperation, I flung them in Art's direction.

"That was good!" he gargled when we both came up for air, neither of us having quite got the hand of snorkel-breathing yet. "Throw some more about three feet in front of me."

So I did. And Art's flash flashed while dozens of fish swarmed in front of him. But enough chip crumbs had fallen in front of me to attract a small herd of my own whose kissy little mouths started nibbling on *my face* when the chips ran out. Which is when I cracked up and filled my snorkel with water again and I came sputtering out of the sea like an idiot. I tried to hoist myself into the boat but my hands slipped. They were covered with thick grease, the underwater gift of the fried tortillas.

"Yuck! I'll *never* eat nachos again!" I whaled.

Kona Joe just shrugged and said, "Fish and chips."

Over dinner that night Art confessed that the odds of his getting any halfway decent incidental underwater whale shots were about the same as Pee Wee Herman's chances of guest hosting for Billy Graham. We probably would have had a serious discussion about the situation, but our food arrived and since we happened to have blundered upon the best Thai restaurant in the known universe, neither of us said much after that, being way too busy with our fresh prawn and coconut milk soup, fresh prawns and eggplant, and rice noodles with fresh prawns.

After dinner we drove to the home of yet another photographer pal of Art's who had arranged an entire slide show of other Maui photographers' work, all of which was very good. But the slides that stopped both Art and me cold were some fantastic underwater shots of humpback whales.

"It would take me *years* to get anything that good," Art sighed on the way back to the hotel.

When I awoke the next morning the first thing I saw was whale spout. I had chosen my hotel because guests in waterfront rooms had often reported seeing whales, but this was ridiculous. Whales were exhaling all over the place out there not even a half mile beyond my lanai. I couldn't wait to get back in the boat.

A chilly wind came up almost as soon as we got past Lahaina. The surf slapped itself onto the shore like albino pancake batter and the water crested in little butter tufts. From a distance it was hard to tell if what you were staring at was a whitecap, another boat or a breaching whale.

"This is starting to suck raw dogs," Art proclaimed delicately.

We battled the wind for about half an hour, then, in the strange way of the air and water currents off this pretty island, we entered some sort of inexplicable quiet zone.

"It's the Maui Triangle," Art pronounced. It *was* spooky.

The wind dropped to a playful zephyr, the Pacific reclaimed its name and the boat stopped beating itself up on the waves. Then we heard it. Whale song.

It rose from the sea like the gut-music of some ancient being, faint but powerful. A distant howling and moaning, pleading, bellowing, that slid up your bones and rang in your head like the weirdest wake-up call you've ever heard.

"No word conveys the eeriness of the whale song," Peter Matthiessen wrote in *Blue Meridian,* "tuned by the ages to a purity beyond refining, a sound that man should hear each morning to remind him of the morning of the world."

. . . and remind woman that she is going swimming with a monster in a couple of seconds. I knew it was coming. And I had no choice.

"If you want your story," Kona Joe yelled, "get in the water *now*."

We didn't know exactly where the whale was. We knew he was far enough away to be legal and close enough to be extremely audible—under good conditions, whale song can travel up to five miles underwater. We also knew that this fellow would be hanging upside-down somewhere below, which is the humpback's chosen singing position.

Art and I stripped down to our swimsuits while I privately lamented having eaten so many shrimp the night before. "What if we smell like krill?" I thought.

Fortunately there was no time to think. We threw on our masks, snorkels and flippers, and fell overboard. And I can tell you that your imagined fear of sharks or even whales is nothing, *nothing* compared to the primal terror of a bottomless pit of empty, blue water. Chinese enamel blue. Blue glass blue. Liquid sapphire cooling steel gas flame blue. There is surely no other blue in this universe like it.

There were also no points of reference. Just the white underbelly of the boat that looked especially insignificant with all that water beneath it. There is, in fact, just you and the endless, subaquatic, Hawaiian blue nothing into which you have been foolish enough to hurl your shrinking pink body.

"Put your head under the water!" Kona Joe cried, seeing that I had already resurfaced.

I did. And the high, wild singing we had heard from the boat suddenly dropped several dozen octaves. The sea, indeed, serves as a giant echo chamber for the water scale of whale music. Its delirious notes played my ribs like a xylophone. I felt as though I myself had become the sound and the sound was everything, a terrific confusion of the senses that allows us to slip out of our known boundaries and into that still, hot place where Einstein's indestructible energy lives. If this is the mating call of the humpback, God only knows what their matehood is like.

As abruptly as the singing started it stopped. Art and I fought for position on the bottom of the ladder.

"This is not my domain," concluded the man who gladly snaps pictures three feet from drooling grizzly bears. Through his snorkel it sounded like he was ordering Chinese food.

By the time we hauled our bodies back on board, I was shaking with fear, excitement and an overdose of undifferentiated electricity. I had heard a whale and he had, most certainly, heard me. I wondered if I had, in fact, been rhymed to.

Whatever I heard, it shall never be heard again, not that song sung that way, because whale music is a living thing created deep in the mysterious four-layered brain of the humpback whose mind has been evolving some sixty-three million years longer than our own.

Back in Lahaina it was business as usual. Overcooked tourists bought "Eat Now, Diet To-Maui" T-shirts while mutant algae creeped down the beach. But later that evening traffic backed up from one end of West Maui to the other. A mother humpback and her new baby were cruising along Lahaina Harbor, very close to shore.

I, of course, watched the whole thing from the box seats on my lanai. The mother swam as slowly as she could but the little one kept falling behind. Their twin exhalations hung in the air like question marks begging the question: Will we manage to protect these wise, old beings from the folly of our ways soon enough to learn the lessons held for us still in their ancient minds? Did the whale spit out Jonah because it disapproved of his prophecies or because *it* read *his* future and seeing a kinder, gentler possibility, decided to give us a second chance?

FADE TO BLACK
BROCK LITTLE

Two years ago I had what was probably the best session of my life, at Waimea Bay. I didn't catch any really great waves, but what I saw and experienced will be with me forever.

I could hear the surf pounding that morning from my house at Pupukea Heights, about two miles from the ocean. It's a common noise when the waves are over 15', so I wasn't afraid—just ready to go. I figured the Quiksilver/Eddie Aikau Memorial contest might be on, so I was a bit stressed to hurry up and get down to the Bay. I had some cereal, grabbed some trunks and walked to my truck.

Unfortunately, my Waimea boards at that time sucked. I had a couple of new 8'3"s that didn't look right. I don't know . . . they were too thin or too light. Something just looked wrong on both of them. One board was clear, the other green and yellow, and I chose the one that had my color (I was born on St. Patrick's Day, and figured the green would bring me luck).

It was still early when I got down to the parking lot at the Bay. No one was around but George Downing, meet director, who was sitting in the lifeguard tower. He's been there for the past three years whenever there's a swell, counting and timing the waves. And every time he eventually decides to postpone the contest. He hasn't blown a call yet.

The surf was about 15–18'—not big enough for the contest, but fun-looking, just the same. Darrick Doerner, always the first guy out at Waimea, was picking off some good ones. It's funny: I've always wanted to get out there before him, but I've never even come close. He must paddle out when it's pitch-dark. Anyway, Darrick was taking off deep as usual, and doing all the right things. He's one of the greatest at Waimea, and gets very little credit.

I talked to George for a while. He said the waves were supposed to be huge, but the swell hadn't arrived yet. I told him it was already pretty big. He assured me it was going to get bigger.

"Are you going to have the contest?" I asked. "Wait and see," he replied. I've been getting that same answer for three years.

More people began to arrive: Foo-Man, James Jones, Cheyne and others—not to mention a bunch of alternates trying to get in the contest. The waves were slowly building. It was about 20' now, and it began to look like the event would be held. I didn't feel like hanging out with a bunch of egotistical big-wave riders, even though most of them are my friends, so I decided to go surfing.

As I walked through the grass to the beach a really big wave came through, at least 21–22'. This is going to be fun, I thought. It wasn't very crowded and Darrick had already come in, so I knew I could get a lot of waves. When I got down to the corner of the Bay I could see the sandbank was extending pretty far out, which meant it would be a hassle getting into the channel. But I figured I could just sink under the waves on my 8'3" and not worry about getting dumped.

A set was rolling up the beach before I could jump in, so I watched and waited. For some reason, just before I paddle out the waves always look a lot bigger than they really are. When the set was finally over I looked out to the horizon. All clear. The next wave hit the beach and rushed up the sand, and I ran down, hit the deck and started paddling. I didn't get very far. The sandbar caused the next wave to dump in front of me. I decided to bail, not dunk under. If I had dunked, I probably would've been washed back up the beach. I always feel stupid when that happens. Instead of paddling out "hair dry" and feeling good, I paddle out with sand in my ears, feeling dumb. Fortunately, only one more wave broke on me—I recovered and was on my way.

The paddle out at Waimea is a lot farther than it looks, and the anxiety and tension build the whole way. I usually feel calm and mellow on the beach, but once I start paddling I realize what I'm getting into. I always try to go alone. On the day the waves had a weird vibe to them—I could feel the power just paddling out. It was strange, though; it was still just 20–22', and totally in control. When I got to the lineup my mind sort of went blank. I didn't feel like talking to anyone, plus I didn't see anybody I liked, so I just sat by myself.

I like to sit deep and to the inside. I lined up with the deepest guy. I'm not sure who it was, but I was about 10 yards to his right. The first set I saw was about 18', and I got the first wave. The drop was basic and the wall was easy. Still, my board felt thin and narrow. I can't really tell how a board works on its first wave, but I can get a feeling— and unfortunately, I was getting a bad one this time. I paddled back out, hoping I was wrong.

After catching a couple of waves the tension I'd felt earlier started coming back. The ocean felt so weird . . . really strong and powerful. When a huge set hit the horizon— way bigger than the other sets—I wasn't surprised at all.

When humongous waves move in I can feel anticipation run across my entire body. So much adrenaline pumps through that sometimes I just yell—or I shake my arms, legs and head to get rid of the jitters. This set was going to be big, but I could tell the waves would be rideable. The first one stood up across the Bay: it didn't look too big, about 22'. No one seemed interested, so Michael Ho led the pack over to the next wave. I swung around and took off on the first one. It was good. Big, but not giant . . . radical, but not insane. I was feeling alright when I kicked out.

Then I saw the beast of a wave behind me. It stood up straight, all the way across the Bay, at least three stories high. I wasn't sure if I should paddle in or paddle out. I didn't particularly want this wave breaking on me. Then I noticed someone at the top, paddling and kicking to get into the thing. It was Michael Ho.

Now, everyone knows Mike's a legendary professional surfer, but he isn't very tall, and he isn't really known for his Waimea ability. Yet there he was, paddling into one of the biggest waves I'd ever seen. Mike *really* wanted that bastard. Almost anyone else who surfs Waimea would've just pulled back, but he was going for it.

The wave was actually trying to break outside the reef, but it just kept feathering. Mike was probably blind from all the spray when he stood up. Lucky thing, too, 'cause he was facing down about 50' to the bottom. Just after Mike got to his feet, the wave finally hit the reef and squared up. He shot down the face, but it was pretty bumpy. I'm not sure why, though—there wasn't much wind.

I don't think Mike was comfortable on his board, because he rode it like a bull: not sure what it was going to do next, and holding on for dear life. About three-quarters of the way down he hit a chop that threw him off the deck. When waves are that big you're going so fast—and so much water is moving up the face—that it's really hard to penetrate the surface. Not only did Mike not penetrate when he hit, he bounced about 3–4' back into the air. It looked like he could've bounced back onto his board. He skipped a little more on the wave face when he landed the second time, then finally broke through the surface . . . ready for another ride to begin.

I had been yelling my lungs out during Michael's entire ride—I *had* to yell, I couldn't stop myself. It was a funny feeling. By the time he'd fallen, though, I had begun to laugh really loud. It was a weird high . . . adrenaline is a radical drug.

After all that yelling and laughing I wasn't ready for the wave to hit me, and I was still laughing when it did, so I didn't get much of a breath. Although I was getting worked and didn't really have enough oxygen, I knew it would be fine, compared to what Mike was going through. I was in the channel where it was mushy, not in the pit.

I was done laughing when I came up, and began to worry about Mike. He popped up just as I was about to paddle over to look for him. He had a startled look, then broke into a huge smile. He'd just ridden what had to be the biggest wave of his life—the ultimate high.

I paddled back out, knowing the waves were building, hoping I could catch a wave like Mike's. Nothing huge came for the next 20 minutes, however, so I just caught a few medium-sized ones. Then the horizon shifted big-time, and I knew something huge was coming.

When it arrived in the Bay, the set looked as major as the last one. Once again, everybody paddled over the first one, and I decided to take it. This time when I kicked out, though, I was pretty much freaked: There was a huge, black, monstrous wave, lined up end-to-end across the Bay, covering the horizon, about to close out.

I was excited, not scared. I hadn't yet had the full-on Waimea experience. I've always wanted to be out when it's closing top-to-bottom, and now that it was about to happen I was really happy.

I saw Dennis Pang make it over the top of the first wave, then it broke right in front of me. I figure the thing was 32–35'. I took two or three deep breaths before my final, full-on breath, then slid off the side of my board. The wave came over and began to take me for a spin. It wasn't too bad: I was in deep water, and although the wave broke top-to-bottom, it didn't grab me that hard. When I came up I was feeling so good that when I saw one more, it didn't bother me.

Here we go again, I thought, as I took another deep breath. Up from wave number two, though, I saw another close-out. I was still pretty comfortable, but not as happy as I'd been a few moments earlier. Also, until I bailed under the third wave I didn't realize how far I'd been dragged.

I hadn't really taken a full-on breath because I was feeling too cocky after the first couple of waves—but soon enough I realized I'd been washed onto a sandbar near the middle of the Bay. After the wave had broken on the out-side, all the whitewater had been rejuvenated when it felt the sandbar bottom, and was taking its newfound energy out on me. I was tired when I surfaced, but doing okay. I looked back and saw my board was broken, but figured it didn't really matter because the board was a piece of shit, anyway. I was a little bummed, though, 'cause I didn't have a good backup for later. While all this was going on I was getting ready for wave number four. And I was no longer enjoying the experience.

The fourth wave worked me harder than the third one had—I was really fighting for air. I usually try to cruise underwater for about five seconds then fight for the top, but this fourth wave had me going. I still wasn't in any real trouble after I came up, so I just looked around and analyzed the situation: I was slowly moving in toward the rocks on the Haleiwa side of the Bay. I figured I wouldn't get there for about six or seven more waves, so that wasn't a threat. Besides, I'd probably drown before I got that far, anyway. I took off my leash, because what was left of my board was pulling me in and holding me back. I began taking more deep breaths for wave number five.

Ken Bradshaw once told me that if a person uses a lot of oxygen going under waves, after about three or four, his lungs don't get as much air. I didn't really believe him until just then. I thought I was ready for the fifth wave, but I wasn't—I began to get tumbled right after I ducked under. I was trying to stay calm, but after a couple of seconds I started fighting, which didn't do me any good; it just caused my body to lose oxygen. I couldn't climb my leash, so I wasn't even sure if I was struggling toward the surface.

I began to feel real mellow, seeing red stars or dots in front of my eyes. It felt kind of good to relax, because I didn't have much power left in me to fight anymore. I knew there was a possibility I'd black out, and if I did I would die. It was a weird feeling . . . I think I know what it would be like to drown: a desperate fight, then peacefulness as you black out. Anyway, I didn't feel like dying, and I'm not so sure I was that close—when I tried to go for the surface again, my body had more fight left than I thought. When I came up I saw another wave.

I've always had this attitude that I would die believing I was going to live. When I went under the sixth wave I knew I would live. I did everything right: took a deep breath, didn't panic, and started fighting after about five seconds. I think I saw red dots again, but by then I wasn't thinking very clearly, so I don't remember.

The seventh wave barely closed out the Bay. After what I'd already been through, I knew this one was going to be easy. I was relaxed as I went under, and prayed this was the last wave of the set. When I came up I was about 30 yards from shore, and although that sounds pretty close, swimming in didn't cross my mind. I took some deep breaths—I wanted to know what it felt like to breathe again. Then I swam out as fast as I could, and stopped when I was far enough out to feel comfortable.

I took another breather, then looked at the surfers across the Bay, and at the traffic along Kam Highway. I saw somebody running up the beach with my board, looking around the whole Bay. I also got a feeling of awe. I often get that feeling at Waimea . . . like some greater spirit is out there watching.

I was in the middle of the Bay, with a really good, natural high running through me. I wanted to float around some more, but I knew I should start moving. I swam over to the Sunset side of the Bay and saw Cheyne. We had a quick conversation about how good the waves were, and how I was feeling. I told him I was fine, but it was time to get going.

I began to swim toward the beach, aiming for the Point, and hoped another set wasn't moving in. I've heard stories of Bradshaw having to swim two or three times around the Bay before being able to safely come in. Once was enough for me.

Luckily, the waves were relatively small as they broke behind me and washed me in. I was staying close to the surface and letting the waves roll me to shore. As I passed the Point I was pretty close to the rocks, right where I wanted to be. If I drifted too far the current would take me into the middle of the shorebreak, and that would mean I'd have to swim around again. I stayed as close to the rocks as I could, and made good progress. When I was about 25 yards from the beach I began to sprint. The current was really strong and tried to take me into the shorebreak, like I'd thought it would. I used the rest of my energy to fight my way to the beach.

I could barely walk up the sand, but my brother was there waiting for me with half my board. I didn't want to fall flat on my face and look stupid in front of him. He began telling me how dumb I was to go out there, and how I could've died. I just smiled.

From that day on I was one of the Big Boys at Waimea—or at least that's what people told me. I don't surf to be in the Big Boys' Club, and I never really needed to be accepted. I just surf Waimea because it's fun. One thing, though: For all those years I heard people talking about big waves being a life-or-death deal, and I never really believed it. Now I do.

IN THE ABYSS
H. G. WELLS

The lieutenant stood in front of the steel sphere and gnawed a piece of pine splinter. "What do you think of it, Steevens?" he asked.

"It's an idea," said Steevens, in the tone of one who keeps an open mind.

"I believe it will smash—flat," said the lieutenant.

"He seems to have calculated it all out pretty well," said Steevens, still impartial.

"But think of the pressure," said the lieutenant. "At the surface of the water it's fourteen pounds to the inch, thirty feet down it's double that; sixty, treble; ninety, four times; nine hundred, forty times; five thousand, three hundred—that's a mile–it's two hundred and forty times fourteen pounds; that's—let's see—thirty hundredweight—a ton and half, Steevens; *a ton and a half* to the square inch. And the ocean where's he's going is five miles deep. That's seven and a half——"

"Sounds a lot," said Steevens, "but it's jolly thick steel."

The lieutenant made no answer, but resumed his pine splinter. The object of their conversation was a huge ball of steel, having an exterior diameter of perhaps nine feet. It looked like the shot for some Titanic piece of artillery. It was elaborately nested in a monstrous scaffolding built into the framework of the vessel, and the gigantic spars that were presently to sling it overboard gave the stern of the ship an appearance that had raised the curiosity of every decent sailor who had sighted it, from the Pool of London to the Tropic of Capricorn. In two places, one above the other, the steel gave place to a couple of circular windows of enormously thick glass, and one of these, set in a steel frame of great solidity, was now partially unscrewed. Both the men had seen the interior of this globe for the first time that morning. It was elaborately padded with air cushions, with little studs sunk between bulging pillows to work the simple mechanism of the affair. Everything was elaborately padded, even the Myers apparatus which was to absorb carbonic acid and replace the oxygen inspired by its tenant, when he had crept in by the glass manhole, and had been screwed in. It was so elaborately padded that a man might have been fired from a gun in it with perfect safety. And it had need to be, for presently a man was to crawl in through that glass manhole, to be screwed up tightly, and to be flung overboard, and to sink down—down—down, for five miles, even as the lieutenant said. It had taken the strongest hold of his imagination; it made him a bore at mess; and he found

Steevens, the new arrival aboard, a godsend to talk to about it, over and over again.

"It's my opinion," said the lieutenant, "that that glass will simply bend in and bulge and smash, under a pressure of that sort. Daubrée has made rocks run like water under big pressures—and, you mark my words——"

"If the glass did break in," said Steevens, "what then?"

"The water would shoot in like a jet of iron. Have you ever felt a straight jet of high pressure water? It would hit as hard as a bullet. It would simply smash him and flatten him. It would tear down his throat, and into his lungs; it would blow in his ears——"

"What a detailed imagination you have!" protested Steevens, who saw things vividly.

"It's a simple statement of the inevitable," said the lieutenant.

"And the globe?"

"Would just give out a few little bubbles, and it would settle down comfortable against the day of judgment, among the oozes and the bottom clay—with poor Elstead spread over his own smashed cushions like butter over bread."

He repeated this sentence as though he liked it very much. "Like butter over bread," he said.

"Having a look at the jigger?" said a voice, and Elstead stood behind them, spick and span in white, with a cigarette between his teeth, and his eyes smiling out of the shadow of his ample hat brim. "What's that about bread and butter, Weybridge? Grumbling as usual about the insufficient pay of naval officers? It won't be more than a day now before I start. We are to get the slings ready today. This clean sky and gentle swell is just the kind of thing for swinging off a dozen tons of lead and iron, isn't it?"

"It won't affect you much," said Weybridge.

"No. Seventy or eighty feet down, and I shall be there in a dozen seconds, there's not a particle moving, though the wind shriek itself hoarse up above, and the water lifts halfway to the clouds. No. Down there"—He moved to the side of the ship and the other two followed him. All three leant forward on their elbows and stared down into the yellow-green water.

"*Peace*," said Elstead, finishing his thought aloud.

"Are you dead certain that clockwork will act?" asked Weybridge presently.

"It has worked thirty-five times," said Elstead. "It's bound to work."

"But if it doesn't."

"Why shouldn't it?"

"I wouldn't go down in that confounded thing," said Weybridge, "for twenty thousand pounds."

"Cheerful chap you are," said Elstead, and spat sociably at a bubble below.

"I don't understand yet how you mean to work the thing," said Steevens.

"In the first place, I'm screwed into the sphere," said Elstead, "and when I've turned the electric light off and on three times to show I'm cheerful, I'm swung out over the stern by that crane, with all those big lead sinkers slung below me. The top lead weight has a roller carrying a hundred fathoms of strong cord rolled up, and that's all that joins the sinkers to the sphere, except the slings that will be cut when the affair is dropped. We use cord rather than wire rope because it's easier to cut and more buoyant— necessary points, as you will see.

"Through each of these lead weights you notice there is a hole, and an iron rod will be run through that and will project six feet on the lower side. If that rod is rammed up from below, it knocks up a lever and sets the clockwork in motion at the side of the cylinder on which the cord winds.

"Very well. The whole affair is lowered gently into the water, and the slings are cut. The sphere floats—with the air in it, it's lighter than water,—but the lead weights go down straight and the cord runs out. When the cord is all paid out, the sphere will go down too, pulled down by the cord."

"But why the cord?" asked Steevens. "Why not fasten the weights directly to the sphere?"

"Because of the smash down below. The whole affair will go rushing down, mile after mile, at a headlong pace at last. It would be knocked to pieces on the bottom if it wasn't for that cord. But the weights will hit the bottom, and directly they do, the buoyancy of the sphere will come into play. It will go on sinking slower and slower; come to a stop at last, and then begin to float upward again.

"That's where the clockwork comes in. Directly the weights smash against the sea bottom, the rod will be knocked through and will kick up the clockwork, and the cord will be rewound on the reel. I shall be lugged down to the sea bottom. There I shall stay for half an hour, with the electric light on, looking about me. Then the clockwork will release a spring knife, the cord will be cut, and up I shall rush again, like a soda-water bubble. The cord itself will help the flotation."

"And if you should chance to hit a ship?" said Weybridge.

"I should come up at such a pace, I should go clean through it," said Elstead, "like a cannon ball. You needn't worry about that."

"And suppose some nimble crustacean should wriggle into your clockwork——"

"It would be a pressing sort of invitation for me to stop," said Elstead, turning his back on the water and staring at the sphere.

They had swung Elstead overboard by eleven o'clock. The day was serenely bright and calm, with the horizon lost in haze. The electric glare in the little upper compartment beamed cheerfully three times. Then they let him down slowly to the surface of the water, and a sailor in the stern chains hung ready to cut the tackle that held the lead weights and the sphere together. The globe, which had looked so large on deck, looked the smallest thing conceivable under the stern of the ship. It rolled a little, and its two dark windows, which floated uppermost, seemed like eyes turned up in round wonderment at the people who crowded the rail. A voice wondered how Elstead liked the rolling. "Are you ready?" sang out the commander. "Ay, ay, sir!" "Then let her go!"

The rope of the tackle tightened against the blade and was cut, and an eddy rolled over the globe in a grotesquely helpless fashion. Someone waved a handkerchief, someone else tried an ineffectual cheer, a middy was counting slowly, "Eight, nine, ten!" Another roll, then with a jerk and a splash the thing righted itself. It seemed to be stationary for a moment, to grow rapidly smaller, and then the water closed over it, and it became visible, enlarged by refraction and dinner, below the surface. Before one could count three it had disappeared. There was a flicker of white light far down in the water, that dimmed to a speck and vanished. Then there was nothing but a depth of water going down into blackness, through which a shark was swimming.

Then suddenly the screw of the cruiser began to rotate, the water was speckled, the shark disappeared in a wrinkled confusion, and a torrent of foam rushed across the crystalline clearness that had swallowed up Elstead. "What's the idea?" said one A. B. to another.

"We're going to lay off about a couple of miles, fear he should hit us when he comes up," said his mate.

The ship steamed slowly to her new position. Abroad her almost everyone who was unoccupied remained watching the breathing swell into which the sphere had sunk. For the next half-hour it is doubtful if a word was spoken that did not bear directly or indirectly on Elstead. The December sun was now high in the sky, and the heat very considerable.

"He'll be cold enough down there," said Weybridge. "They say that below a certain depth sea water's always just about freezing."

"Where'll he come up?" asked Steevens. "I've lost my bearings."

"That's the spot," said the commander, who prided himself on his omniscience. He extended a precise finger southeastward. "And this, I reckon, is pretty nearly the moment," he said. "He's been thirty-five minutes."

"How long does it take to reach the bottom of the ocean?" asked Steevens.

"For a depth of five miles, and reckoning—as we did—an acceleration of two feet per second, both ways, is just about three-quarters of a minute."

"Then he's overdue," said Weybridge.

"Pretty nearly," said the commander. "I suppose it takes a few minutes for that cord of his to wind in."

"I forgot that," said Weybridge, evidently relieved.

And then began the suspense. A minute slowly dragged itself out, and the sphere shot out to the water. Another followed, and nothing broke the low oily swell. The sailors explained to one another that little point about the winding-in of the cord. The rigging was dotted with expectant faces. "Come up, Elstead!" called one hairy-chested salt impatiently, and the others caught it up, and shouted as though they were waiting for the curtain of a theatre to rise.

The commander glanced irritably at them.

"Of course, if the acceleration is less than two," he said, "he'll be all the longer. We aren't absolutely certain that was the proper figure. I'm no slavish believer in calculations."

Steevens agreed concisely. No one on the quarter-deck spoke for a couple of minutes. Then Steevens' watch-case clicked.

When, twenty-one minutes after, the sun reached the zenith, they were still waiting for the globe to reappear, and not a man aboard had dared to whisper that hope was dead. It was Weybridge who first gave expression to that realization. He spoke while the sound of eight bells still hung in the air. "I always distrusted that window," he said quietly suddenly to Steevens.

"Good God!" said Steevens; "you don't think——?"

"Well!" said Weybridge, and left the rest to his imagination.

"I'm no great believer in calculations myself," said the commander dubiously, "so that I'm not altogether hopeless yet." And at midnight the gunboat was steaming slowly in a spiral round the spot where the globe had sunk, and the white beam of the electric light fled and halted and swept discontentedly onward again over the waste of phosphorescent waters under the little stars.

"If his window hasn't burst and smashed him," said Weybridge, "then it's a cursed sight worse, for his clockwork has gone wrong, and he's alive now, five miles under our feet, down there in the cold and dark, anchored in that little bubble of his, where never a ray of light has shone or a human being lived, since the waters were gathered together. He's there without food, feeling hungry and thirsty and scared, wondering whether he'll starve or stifle. Which will it be? The Myers apparatus is running out, I suppose. How long do they last?"

"Good heavens!" he exclaimed; "what little things we are! What daring little devils! Down there, miles and miles of water—all water, and all this empty water about us and this sky. Gulfs!" He threw his hands out, and as he did so, a little white streak swept noiselessly up the sky, traveled more slowly, stopped, became a motionless dot, as though a new star had fallen up into the sky. Then it went sliding back again and lost itself amidst the reflections of the stars and the white haze of the sea's phosphorescence.

At the sight he stopped, arm extended and mouth open. He shut his mouth, opened it again, and waved his arms with an impatient gesture. Then he turned, shouted "El-stead ahoy!" to the first watch, and went at a run to Lindley and the searchlight. "I saw him," he said. "Starboard there! His light's on, and he's just shot out of the water. Bring the light round. We ought to see him drifting, when he lifts on the swell."

But they never picked up the explorer until dawn. Then they almost ran him down. The crane was swung out and a boat's crew hooked the chain to the sphere. When they had shipped the sphere, they unscrewed the manhole and peered into the darkness of the interior (for the electric light chamber was intended to illuminate the water about the sphere, and was shut off entirely from its general cavity).

The air was very hot within the cavity, and the india rubber at the top of the manhole was soft. There was no answer to their eager questions and no sound of movement within. Elstead seemed to be lying motionless, crumpled up in the bottom of the globe. The ship's doctor crawled in and lifted him out to the men outside. For a moment or so they did not know whether Elstead was alive or dead. His face, in the yellow light of the ship's lamps, glistened with perspiration. They carried him down to his own cabin.

He was not dead, they found, but in a state of absolute nervous collapse, and besides cruelly bruised. For some days he had to lie perfectly still. It was a week before he could tell his experiences.

Almost his first words were that he was going down again. The sphere would have to be altered, he said, in order to allow him to throw off the cord if need be, and that was all. He had had the most marvelous experience. "You thought I should find nothing but ooze," he said. "You laughed at my explorations, and I've discovered a new world!" He told his story in disconnected fragments, and chiefly from the wrong end, so that it is impossible to re-tell it in his words. But what follows is the narrative of his experience.

It began atrociously, he said. Before the cord ran out, the thing kept rolling over. He felt like a frog in a football. He could see nothing but the crane and the sky overhead, with an occasional glimpse of the people on the ship's rail. He couldn't tell a bit which way the thing would roll next. Suddenly he would find his feet going up, and try to step, and over he went rolling, head over heels, and just anyhow, on the padding. Any other shape would have been more comfortable, but no other shape was to be relied upon under the huge pressure of the nethermost abyss.

Suddenly the swaying ceased; the globe righted, and when he had picked himself up, he saw the water all about him greeny-blue, with an attenuated light filtering down from above, and a shoal of little floating things went rushing up past him, as it seemed to him, towards the light. And even as he looked, it grew darker and darker, until the water above was as dark as the midnight sky, albeit of a greener shade, and the water below black. And little transparent things in the water developed a faint glint of luminosity, and shot past him in faint greenish streaks.

And the feeling of falling! It was just like the start of a lift, he said, only it kept on. One has to imagine what that means, that keeping on. It was then of all times that Elstead repented of his adventure. He saw the chances against him in an altogether new light. He thought of the big cuttle-fish people knew to exist in the middle waters, the kind of things they find half digested in whales at times, or floating dead and rotten and half eaten by fish. Suppose one caught hold and wouldn't let go. And had the clockwork really been sufficiently tested? But whether he wanted to go on or to go back mattered not the slightest now.

In fifty seconds everything was as black as night outside, except where the beam from his light struck through the waters, and picked out every now and then some fish or scrap of sinking matter. They flashed by too fast for him to see what they were. Once he thinks he passed a shark. And then the sphere began to get hot by friction against the water. They had under-estimated this, it seems.

The first thing he noticed was that he was perspiring, and then he heard a hissing growing louder under his feet, and saw a lot of little bubbles—very little bubbles they were—rushing upward like a fan through the water outside. Steam! He felt the window, and it was hot. He turned on the minute glow-lamp that lit his own cavity, looked at the paddle watch by the studs, and saw he had been travelling now for two minutes. It came into his head that the window would crack through the conflict of temperatures, for he knew the bottom water is very near freezing.

Then suddenly the floor of the sphere seemed to press against his feet, the rush of bubbles outside grew slower and slower, and the hissing diminished. The sphere rolled a little. The window had not cracked, nothing had given, and he knew that the dangers of sinking, at any rate, were over.

In another minute or so he would be on the floor of the abyss. He thought, he said, of Steevens and Weybridge and the rest of them five miles overhead, higher to him than the very highest clouds that ever floated over land are to us, steaming slowly and staring down and wondering what had happened to him.

He peered out of the window. There were no more bubbles now, and the hissing had stopped. Outside there was a heavy blackness—as black as black velvet—except where the electric light pierced the empty water and showed the colour of it—a yellow-green. Then three things like shapes of fire swam into sight, following each other through the water. Whether they were little and near or big and far off he could not tell.

Each was outlined in a bluish light almost as bright as the lights of a fishing smack, a light which seemed to be smoking greatly, and all along the sides of them were specks of this, like the lighter portholes of a ship. Their phosphorescence seemed to go out as they came within the radiance of his lamp, and he saw then that they were little fish of some strange sort, with huge heads, vast eyes, and swindling bodies and tails. Their eyes were turned towards him, and he judged they were following him down. He supposed they were attracted by his glare.

Presently others of the same sort joined them. As he went on down, he noticed that the water became of a pallid colour, and that little specks twinkled in his ray like motes in a sunbeam. This was probably due to the clouds of ooze and mud that the impact of his leaden sinkers had disturbed.

By the time he was drawn down to the lead weights he was in a dense fog of white that his electric light failed altogether to pierce for more than a few yards, and many minutes elapsed before the hanging sheets of sediment subsided to any extent. Then, lit by his light and by the transient phosphorescence of a distant shoal of fishes, he was able to see under the huge blackness of the super-incumbent water an undulating expanse of greyish-white ooze, broken here and there by tangled thickets of a growth of sea lilies, waving hungry tentacles in the air.

Farther away were the graceful, translucent outlines of a group of gigantic sponges. About this floor there were scattered a number of bristling flattish tufts of rich purple and black, which he decided must be some sort of sea-urchin, and small, large-eyed or blind things having a curious resemblance, some to woodlice, and others to lobsters, crawled sluggishly across the track of the light and vanished into the obscurity again, leaving furrowed trails behind them.

Then suddenly the hovering swarm of little fishes veered about and came towards him as a flight of starlings might do. They passed over him like a phosphorescent snow, and then he saw behind them some larger creature advancing towards the sphere.

At first he could see it only dimly, a faintly moving figure remotely suggestive of a walking man, and then it came into the spray of light that the lamp shot out. As the glare struck it, it shut its eyes, dazzled. He stared in rigid astonishment.

It was a strange vertebrated animal. Its dark purple head was dimly suggestive of a chameleon, but it had such a high forehead and such a braincase as no reptile ever displayed before; the vertical pitch of its face gave it a most extraordinary resemblance to a human being.

Two large and protruding eyes projected from sockets in chameleon fashion, and it had a broad reptilian mouth with hoary lips beneath its little nostrils. In the position of the ears were two huge gill-covers, and out of these floated a branching tree of coralline filaments, almost like the tree-like gills that very young rays and sharks possess.

But the humanity of the face was not the most extraordinary thing about the creature. It was a biped; its almost globular body was poised on a tripod of two frog-like legs and a long thick tail, and its forelimbs, which grotesquely caricatured the human hand, much as a frog's do, carried a long shaft of bone, tipped with copper. The colour of the creature was variegated; its head, hands, and legs were purple; but its skin, which hung loosely upon it, even as clothes might do, was a phosphorescent grey. And it stood there blinded by the light.

At last this unknown creature of the abyss blinked its eyes open, and shading them with its disengaged hand, opened its mouth, and gave vent to a shouting noise, articulate almost as speech might be, that penetrated even the steel case and padded jacket of the sphere. How a shouting may be accomplished without lungs Elstead does not profess to explain. It then moved sideways out of the glare into the mystery of shadow that bordered it on either side, and Elstead felt rather than saw that it was coming towards him. Fancying the light had attracted it, he turned the switch that cut off the current. In another moment something soft dabbed upon the steel, and the globe swayed.

Then the shouting was repeated, and it seemed to him that a distant echo answered it. The dabbing recurred, and the globe swayed and ground against the spindle over which the wire was rolled. He stood in the blackness and peered out into the everlasting night of the abyss. And presently he saw, very faint and remote, other phosphorescent quasi-human forms hurrying towards him.

Hardly knowing what he did, he felt about in his swaying prison for the stud of the exterior electric light, and came by accident against his own small glow-lamp in its padded recess. The sphere twisted, and then threw him down; he heard shouts like shouts of surprise, and when he rose to his feet, he saw two pairs of stalked eyes peering into the lower window and reflecting his light.

In another moment hands were dabbing vigorously at his steel casing, and there was a sound, horrible enough in his position, of the metal protection of the clockwork being vigorously hammered. That, indeed, sent his heart into his mouth, for if these strange creatures succeeded in stopping that, his release would never occur. Scarcely had he thought as much when he felt the sphere sway violently, and the floor of it press hard against his feet. He turned off the small glow-lamp that lit the interior, and sent the ray of the large light in the separate compartment out into the water. The sea-floor and the man-like creatures had disappeared, and a couple of fish chasing each other dropped suddenly by the window.

He thought at once that these strange denizens of the deep sea had broken the rope, and that he had escaped. He drove up faster and faster, and then stopped with a jerk that sent him flying against the padded roof of his prison. For half a minute, perhaps, he was too astonished to think.

Then he felt that the sphere was spinning slowly, and rocking, and it seemed to him that it was also being drawn through the water. By crouching close to the window, he managed to make his weight effective and roll that part of the sphere downward, but he could see nothing save the pale ray of his light striking down ineffectively into the darkness. It occurred to him that he would see more if he turned the lamp off, and allowed his eyes to grow accustomed to the profound obscurity.

In this he was wise. After some minutes the velvety blackness became a translucent blackness, and then, far away, and as faint as the zodiacal light of an English summer evening, he saw shapes moving below. He judged these creatures had detached his cable, and were towing him along the sea bottom.

And then he saw something faint and remote across the undulations of the submarine plain, a broad horizon of pale luminosity that extended this way and that way as far as the range of his little window permitted him to see. To this he was being towed, as a balloon might be towed by men out of the open country into a town. He approached it very slowly, and very slowly the dim irradiation was gathered together into more definite shapes.

It was nearly five o'clock before he came over this luminous area, and in that time he could make out an arrangement suggestive of streets and houses grouped about a vast roofless erection that was grotesquely suggestive of a ruined abbey. It was spread out like a map below him. The houses were all roofless enclosures of walls, and their substance being, as he afterwards saw, of phosphorescent bones, gave the place an appearance as if it were built of drowned moonshine.

Among the inner caves of the place waving trees of crinoid stretched their tentacles, and tall, slender, glassy sponges shot like shining minarets and lilies of filmy light out of the general glow of the city. In the open spaces of the place he could see a stirring movement as of crowds of people, but he was too many fathoms above them to distinguish the individuals in those crowds.

Then slowly they pulled him down, and as they did so, the details of the place crept slowly upon his apprehension. He saw that the courses of the cloudy buildings were marked out with beaded lines of round objects, and then he perceived that at several points below him, in broad open spaces, were forms like the encrusted shapes of ships.

Slowly and surely he was drawn down, and the forms below him became brighter, clearer, more distinct. He was being pulled down, he perceived, towards the large building in the centre of the town, and he could catch a glimpse ever and again of the multitudinous forms that were lugging at his cord. He was astonished to see that the rigging of one of the ships, which formed such a prominent feature of the place, was crowded with a host of gesticulating figures regarding him, and then the walls of the great building rose about him silently, and hid the city from his eyes.

And such walls they were, of water-logged wood, and twisted wire-rope, and iron spars, and copper, and the bones and skulls of dead men. The skulls ran in zigzag lines and spirals and fantastic curves over the building; and in and out of their eye-sockets, and over the whole surface of the place, lurked and played a multitude of silvery little fishes.

Suddenly his ears were filled with a low shouting and a noise like the violent blowing of horns, and this gave place to a fantastic chant. Down the sphere sank, past the huge pointed windows, through which he saw vaguely a great number of these strange, ghostlike people regarding him, and at last he came to rest, as it seemed, on a kind of altar that stood in the centre of the place.

And now he was at such a level that he could see these strange people of the abyss plainly once more. To his astonishment, he perceived that they were prostrating themselves before him, all save one, dressed as it seemed in a robe of placoid scales, and crowned with a luminous diadem who stood with his reptilian mouth opening and shutting, as though he led the chanting of the worshippers.

A curious impulse made Elstead turn on his small globe-lamp again, so that he became visible to these creatures of the abyss, albeit the glare made them disappear forthwith into night. At this sudden sight of him, the chanting gave place to a tumult of exultant shouts; and Elstead, being anxious to watch them, turned his light off again, and vanished from before their eyes. But for a time he was too blind to make out what they were doing, and when at last he could distinguish them, they were kneeling again. And thus they continued worshipping him, without rest or intermission, for a space of three hours.

Most circumstantial was Elstead's account of this astounding city and its people, these people of perpetual night, who have never seen sun or moon or stars, green vegetation, nor any living, air-breathing creatures who know nothing of fire, nor any light but the phosphorescent light of living things.

Startling as is his story, it is yet more startling to find that scientific men, of such eminence as Adams and Jenkins, find nothing incredible in it. They tell me they see no reason why intelligent, water-breathing, vertebrated creatures, inured to a low temperature and enormous pressure, and of such a heavy structure, that neither alive nor dead would they float, might not live upon the bottom of the deep sea, and quite unsuspected by us, descendants like ourselves of the great Theriomorpha of the New Red Sandstone age.

We should be known to them, however, as strange meteoric creatures, wont to fall catastrophically dead out of the mysterious blackness of their watery sky. And not only we ourselves, but our ships, or metals, our appliances, would come raining down out of the night. Sometimes sinking things would smite down and crush them, as if it were the judgment of some unseen power above, and sometimes would come things of the utmost rarity or utility, or shapes of inspiring suggestion. One can understand, perhaps, something of their behavior at the descent of a living man, if one thinks what a barbaric people might do, to whom an enhaloed, shining creature came suddenly out of the sky.

At one time or another Elstead probably told the officers of the *Ptarmigan* every detail of his strange twelve hours in the abyss. That he also intended to write them down is certain, but he never did, and so unhappily we have to piece together the discrepant fragments of his story from the reminiscences of Commander Simmons, Weybridge, Steevens, Lindley and the others.

We see the thing darkly in fragmentary glimpses— the huge ghostly building, the bowing, chanting people, with their dark chameleon-like heads and faintly luminous clothing, and Elstead, with his light turned on again, vainly trying to convey to their minds that the cord by which the sphere was held was to be severed. Minute after minute slipped away, and Elstead, looking at his watch, was horrified to find that he had oxygen only for four hours more. But the chant in his honour kept on as remorselessly as if it was the marching song of his approaching death.

The manner of his release he does not understand, but to judge by the end of cord that hung from the sphere, it had been cut through by rubbing against the edge of the altar. Abruptly the sphere rolled over, and he swept up, out of their world, as an ethereal creature clothed in a vacuum would sweep through our own atmosphere back to its native tether again. He must have torn out of their sight as a hydrogen bubble hastens upward from our air. A strange ascension it must have seemed to them.

The sphere rushed up with even greater velocity than, when weighted with the lead sinkers, it had rushed down. It became exceedingly hot. It drove up with the windows uppermost, and he remembers the torrent of bubbles frothing against the glass. Every moment he expected this to fly. Then suddenly something like a huge wheel seemed to be released in his head, the padded compartment began spinning about him, and he fainted. His next recollection was of his cabin, and of the doctor's voice.

But that is the substance of the extraordinary story that Elstead related in fragments to the officers of the *Ptarmigan*. He promised to write it all down at a later date. His mind was chiefly occupied with the improvement of his apparatus, which was effected at Rio.

It remains only to tell that on February 2, 1896, he made his second descent into the ocean abyss, with the improvements his first experience suggested. What happened we shall probably never know. He never returned. The *Ptarmigan* beat about over the point of his submersion, seeking him in vain for thirteen days. Then she returned to Rio, and the news was telegraphed to his friends. So the matter remains for the present. But it is hardly probable that no further attempt will be made to verify his strange story of these hitherto unsuspected cities of the deep sea.

S.O.S.

BIOGRA

ACKNOWL

PHIES

EDGMENTS

BIOGRAPHIES

John Biguenet is a poet, critic, and author of *The Craft of Translation, Theories of Translation,* and *Foreign Fictions.* His work has appeared in *Granta, Esquire,* and *Joe.*

Julia Blackburn has written several books, including *Daisy Bates in the Desert, The Book of Color,* and *The Leper's Companions.* She is the daughter of British poet Thomas Blackburn and lives in Suffolk, England.

Tim Cahill is a columnist and one of the founding editors of *Outside* magazine, as well as a contributing editor of *Rolling Stone.* His adventure travel writing has been collected in *Jaguars Ripped My Flesh, Pass the Butterworms,* and *A Wolverine Is Eating My Leg.*

Joseph Conrad was born in Poland in 1857 and died in England in 1924. He worked on French ships, entered the British Merchant Service, and traveled widely. His life at sea provided him with much material for works such as *Lord Jim, Nostromo,* and "Heart of Darkness."

Gabriel García Márquez was born in Colombia in 1928 and worked as a journalist in Latin America, Europe, and the United States. His novel *One Hundred Years of Solitude* has won many prizes worldwide.

Ernest Hemingway, born in 1899, is famous for novels such as *The Sun Also Rises, A Farewell to Arms, For Whom the Bell Tolls,* and *The Old Man and the Sea,* for which he won the Pulitzer Prize in fiction in 1953. He won the Nobel Prize for Literature in 1954. He committed suicide in Ketchum, Idaho, in 1961.

Sebastian Junger has written for *Outside, Men's Journal,* and *New York Times Magazine*. He lives in New York City.

Rockwell Kent was an artist as well as an author, whose works were shown widely in America and Europe. His other books include *Wilderness, Voyaging Southward from the Strait of Magellan,* and *Of Men and Mountains*. He died in 1971 at the age of eighty-nine.

Deborah Scaling Kiley was born in Texas and was involved in the Outward Bound program, where she learned many of the skills that helped her survive the shipwreck she writes of in *Albatross*. She lives in Massachusetts with her husband and children.

Stephen King is a modern master of the horror genre, having written many best-selling novels such as *Carrie, Salem's Lot,* and *Tommyknockers*. He was born in Maine and resides there still.

Brock Little is a professional surfer and big-wave legend. He was born in 1967 and lives in Haleiwa, Hawaii.

Jessica Maxwell lives in Oregon and has written for *Audubon, Esquire, Forbes,* and *Travel and Leisure.* She is the author of *I Don't Know Why I Swallowed the Fly: My Fly Fishing Rookie Season.*

Nathaniel Philbrick lives in Nantucket, Massachusetts, where he is the director of the Egan Institute of Maritime Studies and a research fellow at the Nantucket Historical Association. His other books include *Away Off Shore: Nantucket Island and Its People, 1602–1890,* and *Abram's Eyes: The Native American Legacy of Nantucket Island.*

Edgar Allan Poe was born in Boston in 1809. Although he favored poetry, he also wrote novels, book reviews, and essays and became known as the first master of the short-story form. He died in Baltimore in 1849.

Archibald Rutledge was born in 1883 and was poet laureate of South Carolina for many years. He wrote and published poetry and prose since his teens. His books include *Tales of Whitetails* and *Home by the River.* He was a contributor to magazines for half a century, publishing more than a thousand articles and poems.

Neil Simon was born in 1972 and is based in New York City, but often travels the world with his surfboard, scuba, and rock-climbing gear. He is a frequent contributor to *blue magazine.*

Paul Theroux has written many best-selling travel books and novels, including *The Great Railway Bazaar, The Kingdom by the Sea*, and *The Mosquito Coast*. "Rowing Around the Cape" was first published in *Sunrise with Seamonsters*.

H. G. Wells is most famous for his science-fantasy novels. In his seventy-nine years, he wrote more than eighty books, among them *The Invisible Man, The War of the Worlds,* and *The Time Machine*. He died in London in 1946.

Geoffrey Wolff was born in Los Angeles in 1937 and educated at Princeton University. He has written several novels as well as nonfiction, including *The Duke of Deception,* a biography of his father. He currently teaches in the graduate fiction program at the University of California at Irvine.

From *N by E* by Rockwell Kent. Copyright © 1930, 1958 by Rockwell Kent. Reprinted by permission of University Press of New England. From *The Perfect Storm* by Sebastian Junger. Copyright © 1997 by Sebastian Junger. Used by permission of W. W. Norton & Company, Inc. "In a Fog" by Geoffrey Wolff was first published in the August 1988 issue of *Cruising World* magazine. Copyright © 1988 by Geoffrey Wolff. Reprinted by permission of International Creative Management, Inc. "Rowing Around the Cape" from *Sunrise with Seamonsters* by Paul Theroux. Copyright © 1985 by Paul Theroux. Reprinted with the permission of The Wylie Agency, Inc. "Survivor Type" by Stephen King. Copyright © Stephen King. Reprinted with permission. All rights reserved. Excerpt from *Albatross* by Deborah Scaling Kiley and Meg Noonan. Copyright © 1994 by Deborah Scaling Kiley. Reprinted by permission of Houghton Mifflin Co. All rights reserved. From *The Story of a Shipwrecked Sailor* by Gabriel García Márquez. Translation copyright © 1986 by Alfred A. Knopf Inc. Reprinted by permission of Alfred A. Knopf, a Division of Random House Inc. "And Never Come Up" from *The Torturer's Apprentice* by John Biguenet was first published in *Granta 61: The Sea*. Copyright © 2000 by John Biguenet. Reprinted by permission of HarperCollins Publishers, Inc. "The Attack", from *In the Heart of the Sea* by Nathaniel Philbrick. Copyright © 2000 by Nathaniel Philbrick. Reprinted by permission of Viking Penguin, a division of Penguin Putnam. "Death in the Moonlight" by Archibald Rutledge was first published in the 1933 issue of *Field & Stream* magazine. Copyright © 1933 by Archibald Rutledge. Reprinted by permission of Times Mirror Magazines, Inc. "Drunken Diving for Poison Sea Snakes" from *A Wolverine Is Eating My Leg* by Tim Cahill. Copyright © 1989 by Tim Cahill. Reprinted by permission of Vintage Books, a Division of Random House Inc. From *The Old Man and the Sea* by Ernest Hemingway. Copyright © 1952 by Ernest Hemingway. Copyright renewed © 1980 by Mary Hemingway. Reprinted with permission of Scribner, A Division of Simon & Schuster. "The Mermaid" by Julia Blackburn was first published in *Granta 61: The Sea*. Copyright © by Julia Blackburn. Reprinted by permission. "Diving Beyond Limits" by Neil Simon. Copyright © 2000 by Neil Simon. Reprinted by permission of Blue Media Ventures LLC. "Rhapsody in Blue" by Jessica Maxwell. Copyright © 1997 by Jessica Maxwell. Reprinted from *Femme d'Adventure* with permission of Seal Press. "Fade to Black" by Brock Little was first printed in *Surfer* magazine. Reprinted by permission.